1914-1919:
The War Diaries of a
Norfolk Man

* * * * *

William C. Bennett

ARCADE Publishers
2014

1914-1919: The War Diaries of a Norfolk Man: first published 2014 by Arcade Publishers, The Tannery, Frith Lane, Ledbury HR8 1LW, UK.

©Maureen A. Dening on behalf of the descendants of William C. Bennett, 2014.

A catalogue record for this book is available from the British Library.

ISBN 978-0-9560714-2-2

Contents

Illustration

opposite page 208

Portrait of William C. Bennett, after being commissioned as an officer, painted 1919 or later by his brother-in-law Ernest Faircloth.

Introduction
to the present edition

I am the granddaughter of William C. Bennett.
William was born in 1890 and died in 1981 aged
90. On October 30, 1916, he married his girl
friend Elizabeth and they had three daughters:
my mother Doris; Gwendolyn, known as Dee,
mother of my cousin Michael; and Evelyn,
known as Evie, mother of my cousins Drake
and Caroline.

We cousins remember him and our
grandmother well, as they both lived to a great
age and the family were regularly reunited in
Norfolk. We have some recordings of merry
evenings at 40, Woodland Road, Hellesdon,
Norwich, when dear Pop would be teased by
his three daughters and persuaded to sing an old
song.

My mother died last year and I found in her
possessions two good-sized notebooks,
looseleaf and bound together with string and a
bootlace, largely handwritten, with some printed
pages pasted in and with a few drawings and
photographs. The title: *A Norfolk Youth*,
Volumes One and Two, by Wm. Bennett.

We have drawn the present edition of material specific to his experiences in the Great War of 1914-1919 from these notebooks. This year of 2014 marks, after all, the centenary since the outbreak of the war and since William Bennett enlisted.

The original notebooks also include essays on the people and places of Norfolk, some sections, such as "Doings at Diss" or "Early Printing and its Impact on Norwich," being found originally in the book *Looking at Norfolk*, by Jane Hales in collaboration with William Bennett, published in 1971 by Geo. R. Reeve Ltd., Wymondham, Norfolk. William was the author of other works of local interest, including *Some Grim Goings-on in Norfolk* (published 1977, printed by Geo. R. Reeve), a collection of local stories with his own line drawings. William contributed line drawings to another book by Jane Hales, *The East Wind, an Unusual Guide to Norfolk* (1969). He also left local sketches and numerous watercolour paintings.

He recounts his early days as an apprentice printer before the war, becoming a compositor with Fletcher & Son in Norwich. He made good friends with Ernest Faircloth, brother of William's future wife Elizabeth, an artist apprentice at printers Page Bros of Norwich, who sat at the same bench that A J Munnings had used a few years earlier. During the war Ernest Faircloth was to be sent as a cartographer to Mesopotamia; in the family we have some of his watercolours too.

The notebooks are mainly in William Bennett's handwriting, with one or two annotations by his daughter Gwendolyn. The text is an expanded fair copy made in 1974, when William would have been 84, based to some extent on a rough draft of his experiences he made in 1922.

The account is fragmentary and impressionistic, the chronology is often unclear and the hundred-plus pages are far from a systematic account of events. But the effect is dispassionate, truthful, poignant and quite often humorous.

The present edition is presented where possible in parallel form, with the handwritten original in facsimile on the left, and a transcribed text on the right. The transcription preserves as far as possible the format and occasional lapses or inconsistencies of spelling and punctuation. It has been necessary to reduce slightly the size of the handwritten original. The text is presented in the author's original short sections with his titles. We have added section or chapter numbers for clarity.

We have chosen to begin this war memoir with a chapter of material from the original diaries in which William tells something of his early life and experiences before he signed up. This 'introduction' is rich with the local colour of pre-war Norfolk. The early material, which also includes the first months of military service (up to the present chapter 4), was previously typeset and previously published, and these pages of typeset text are founded pasted into the diary pages. These sections have, or may have, variously appeared in: The Eastern Daily Press; in "Norfolk Fair" and "Norfolk Life"; and in Jane Hales' book *Looking at Norfolk*, mentioned above. We cannot attribute all the sources exactly, but we acknowledge and thank the original publishers. We have re-set the text in the present edition.

William Bennett was a brave and stoical – and lucky – man. He enlisted in August 1914, the first month of the war, and served until May 1919. He was wounded and hospitalised more than once. He fought on the Somme and at Passchendaele. He recounts an episode in the aftermath of the battle of the Somme, after the retaking of Delville Wood, when a comrade and

Introduction

he were the only two left of a company of 70
men; whereupon the bullet of a German sniper
passed through his nose and killed the other
man beside him. He recounts seeing a shell fall
a yard from him; it was a dud. He recounts
taking a fragment of shell casing in the thigh; it
was extracted and the wound was dressed; 20
years later, the leg was amputated.

We offer this edition so that our children and
grandchildren and others younger than us may
remember; and as a tribute to the fortitude of a
Norfolk man.

Maureen A Dening
Ledbury, August 2014

Prefatory note
found in the notebooks

The story of "A Norfolk Youth" is the life history of a soldier of the first world war, who served in the 8th Battalion of the Norfolk Regiment from August 22nd, 1914, until he relinquished his commission in 1922, i.e., Wm. Charles Bennett of 40 Woodland Road, Hellesdon, Norwich and written by him.

G M Hart
(daughter), 1974

1. Early days

I was born at Kenninghall in Norfolk on May 25th 1890, but I was only a year old when my family moved to Palgrave, where my father had taken up an appointment as Farm Steward. As our house was not ready, we spent six miserable months in a tiny cottage; the area was frequented by gypsies, a disorderly law-breaking set of people, including some "Diddicoes," mostly travelling tinkers who lived in caravans but were not gypsies. They were expert thieves; in fact, it had been known for two women to call at a house, and as one of them would be engaging the mistress in conversation, the other would be taking the washing off the line. The gypsies would have nothing to do with them and fights between the two sections were common. It was a superstition that they could put a spell on cattle or pigs, so if any farm animals died or contracted a disease after a visit it was put down to them. They peddled cottons, threads, candles and bootlaces and generally people bought one small item at least to avoid their displeasure.

My earliest recollections were of being taken by my mother for an outing in a push-cart – a rather large affair made of wood. I have since wondered how the mothers of the time, in long skirts, managed to push this "chariot" on the very muddy, stony roads. At the time, I was wearing a red and buff outfit, the trousers were kept down by a loop attached and fastened under the boots.

When I was still young my mother took me to see the circus procession through Diss. On one of the decorated vehicles was a lady impersonating "Britannia," with a *real* lion at her feet. Everybody was very thrilled to see the lion lying so quietly on the top of the circus wagon. When the procession arrived on the ground where all the vans were parked, the lion walked about half way down the steps from the tall van, jumped on to the ground and ran around several times before it was caught. Someone shouted "The lion is loose" and, on hearing this, my mother lost no time in getting me home in the push-chair. The lion was an old one and not at all dangerous, but a lion was a lion to country people!

Whenever we, who lived at Palgrave in Suffolk wanted to visit Diss, in Norfolk, it was necessary to pass through an area on the outskirts of the town known as "Denmark." Some of the roughest characters resided there, in 2-roomed cottages of thatch, lath and plaster and the rent was only 2s to 3s a week. There were some who were always behind with their rents, but most of the landlords were very considerate and did not press the matter too far. They led a hand-to-mouth existence, it was almost a question of survival of the fittest. The children who survived were generally "tough" and had a lot of stamina. Once, when my friend and I were crossing the bridge over the river, we were confronted by a couple of hefty lads, who said "Where do you think you're going?" We replied, "Into the town, as far as the Coffee Tavern." "We don't know so much about that," said the lads. Whereupon we struck out, each taking his man, and dashed off, dodging down some passages and by-roads to shake off our pursuers. Similar incidents occurred all the time, and if you should live in Suffolk and have a girl-friend in Norfolk, you would be warned to seek one elsewhere. There would be no second warning, and you would have to fight your way out of the town or village concerned next time such an occasion occurred.

There were army manoeuvres on the commons and heaths nearby, and sometimes units would lie in camp for a month or more during the summer... many a soldier married a local girl.

My school days were interrupted by a year at home suffering from the effects of bronchitis, so my sister taught me to read and write, and gave me lessons in simple arithmetic.

Therefore, I skipped the Primary Classes and commenced my school life in Standard I. They were happy days, with games in which the master took part — football, hockey, cricket, paper-chasing, etc. When the village pond was frozen over for long periods there was plenty of skating and sliding. One day, the Master was doing some rather fancy movements, when he fell, and the ice broke. As he cut a sorry figure emerging from the water, some of the boys laughed, and were reported to the Headmaster by his wife. Later, they were escorted to the Headmaster's room, where punishment was duly carried out. Every Monday morning the Rector would call at the school and take the "assembly." I well remember the ritual. "Good morning, children," and our reply, "Good morning, Sir." He was a bearded man and had a benevolent appearance, but this was misleading. He could be very autocratic, and, on occasions, very overbearing. If you attended church you shared in any benefits which might be going. If you were not a church member you were out of luck when it came to winter-time, and the bequests of coal, which should have been given to all aged people of 70 and over, just didn't come your way. Also, I remember, that one day, whilst returning from school, we were looking for beech-nuts on the bank of a meadow which belonged to Miss Kay, a very nice lady, who always waved to us boys when she passed in her carriage; on this occasion when His Reverence was passing in his gig, with coachman behind, he leaned out and lashed us with his whip. My friend, who was a giant for his age, was mad with rage and ran behind the gig shaking his fist and calling the Parson all the names in the calendar. I thought we should have heard more of this but, fortunately for us the Reverend Gentleman couldn't have heard. The parson was a power in the village, and all the males had to "touch their caps" to him; also all women and girls had to curtsey, calling him all sorts of names after he had passed by!

* * * * *

The head boy of the school used to decide what punishment should be meted out to a junior who had been rude to a senior. There was "running the gauntlet of fire and water;" two ranks of boys faced inwards, and the offender had to run up and down the line three times. If it was "fire" the culprit would be belaboured with knotted handkerchiefs, if "water" was chosen, all the boys would spit at the unfortunate one – a very unpleasant ordeal. If a quarrel broke out between two boys, they were hustled into a circle with boys all round, and had to fight it out and fair play was ensured by the head boy. It was a rough life really.

On the farm, in our leisure hours, the horse-play and other things we did all helped to shape us for adult life. Driving cattle to market and from the train; exercising one of the ponies with a halter and a blanket to sit on, a very precarious seat as I often found before becoming proficient.

The countryman is always portrayed as a "Bumpkin," an ignorant clot, but they liked nothing better than to have a "Towny" staying on the farm, so that they could show him a few things. The Towny would be asked to assist in catching some young owls. His job would be to hold a sieve, using a two-tined fork, up against the slatted aperture at the top of the stable wall, to prevent the owls getting out, whilst the farm boys would go up the ladder inside the stable to collect the owls with a sack. The farm boys carried a pail of water to the loft and called out "Are you ready?" Back came the reply, "Yes," and then the Towny received a shower of water, soaking him to the skin.

When I was 13, my friend, the schoolmaster's son sat for a scholarship, and later attended Eye Grammar School. I had been receiving instruction with Harry with a view to taking the exam too, but my father said it was more important to have a trade. One didn't argue with one's parents in those days, and I was apprenticed to a firm of Printers, called Messrs. Lusher Brothers. They told my father they would make a tradesman of me, and they taught me everything they knew. The first year I was a "Printer's Devil." In the winter months it was very trying. The first duty was to take down the shutters, and light the "Tortoise" stoves. Cinders had to be sifted, and hods of coke filled. Nothing could be printed until the works were warm enough for the ink to move freely on the composition rollers. All this, and cleaning the machines and rollers and gas engine made the Printer's Devil very dirty with ink stains on his face and hands. I had also to run errands, and deliver printed work to customers. It has often been said that "a woman's work is never done," and it was the same with the Printer's Devil.

In the second year I became a slightly superior person, receiving some instruction in the art of printing and by the end of the final year, could operate any machine in the works – a very comprehensive education. I experienced many amusing incidents. Once, at election time, I had to take proofs to the agent of the Unionist party. My masters were Liberals and Non-conformists, but they printed for both sides, in red ink for the Unionists or Torys, and in blue for the Liberals. The agent laid the poster proof out on the table, and read the words on the bill for my benefit. "Vote for Mann (the Tory) printed by a couple of damn good Liberals."

* * * * *

At the termination of my apprenticeship as a printer at Diss, I was offered a job as compositor by Fletcher and Son Ltd. of Castle Works in Davy Place at Norwich, and was driven to the station to catch the train by my friend. I knew I should miss him, and I believe he felt the same about me. After I had settled in Norwich he did visit me now and then, and we never lost touch, even though he went to Australia.

Arriving at Norwich I felt completely overawed by all the hustle and traffic. Leaving my trunk at the station, I made my way to Fletchers, where I met the managing director, Mr Mason. He was a very nice, fatherly type of man and seeing I was nervous, put me at my ease at once by a remark which allayed all my fears. After a chat about the work I should be doing, he introduced me to Mr Turner, one of the Composing room staff, who, he thought might be able to help me in the matter of accommodation. This was providential, as I had no provisions for lodgings, and this man took me to see his mother, and we fixed up things very agreeably, and I stayed there until I joined the army in August, 1914. The date was now November 9th, 1909. Mrs Turner and her husband were good Methodist people; they took me with them to church every Sunday, and later introduced me to some of the young men there, who were full of life and high spirits, and we had a lot of fun together. It was not long before we started a physical culture club in a room over a fish shop in Dereham Road. The shopkeeper was an ex-sailor, and did a lot for us, especially with installing the equipment for our use. Then we formed a football club which was in being till the war broke it up, most of its members joining the Forces. Boating and swimming were other pursuits, and in the summer we would often walk down to the "Eagle" and have a dip about 6 p.m.

One of the members of our "crowd" was Ernest Faircloth, and I became especially attached to him and, living in the same street, we were in close touch. He was an artist apprentice with Page Bros., Back St. Stephen's Street, Norwich. This was the same firm where A. J. Munnings, the well-known artist, served his apprenticeship, and Ernest worked at the same bench which Munnings had used earlier. Munnings was a great inspiration to young students at the Norwich Art School in St. George's Street.

This was a time when the only picture show in Norwich was at the Victoria Hall, St. Stephen's St., and the charge was 2d. There was a man in a bowler hat standing just at the entrance, announcing the titles of films, and, apparently, there was one continuous performance, for whenever one went by, he was always saying, "Now showing." It was a poor show, and one can understand why the name "flicks" caught on; the best seats were just bare forms, and the rest of the audience stood about in groups. It was quite a relief to get out into the air again, as there was a lot of smoking.

Roller skating was very much the vogue at this time, and the "rinkeries" were on the corner where "Delves Motors" building now stands, with dancing nightly to the music of the "Blue Hungarian" band. There were also attractive programmes at the Hippodrome and Theatre. Trams had just been introduced, and there was only an odd car or two in use, and everyone raced off the road if one of those appeared in sight. Hansom cabs and "flys" were still plying for hire, and both had their "ranks" about the city. In summer the "Jenny Lind" paddle-steamer made daily trips to Bramerton "Woods End," and Coldham Hall, and there were concert parties at "The Nest" football ground, Spring Gardens, and the Gardens in Thorpe.

The Norfolk Agricultural Show was held at Crown Point, Whitlingham, in June 1911, and King George and Queen Mary visited Norwich. There was a grand parade in the city when the King rode at the head of the Royal Norfolk Yeomanry in their attractive uniforms. It was a great day for Norwich; Ailwyn Fellowes was knighted by King George in St. Andrew's Hall. Sir Ailwyn lived at Honingham Hall, which was entirely demolished by contractors in 1966. All that perpetuates its memory is a small, ancient building now used as a club.

* * * * *

The city was full of strange characters. There was an odd-job man called "Sugar-me-Sop," and the legendary figure of Spring-heeled Jack, who was said to possess some wonderful shoes which gave him the power to spring long distances. His speciality was to jump from "nowhere at all" down into the midst of card-players seated on the ground on Mousehold Heath; before they had time to recover from their surprise, Spring-heeled Jack would snatch all the money from the "kitty" and disappear with one of his gigantic springs. Mothers used to warn their children to watch out for Spring-heeled-Jack when they went to play on Mousehold. Then there was a woman named Maggie Murphy, a street singer, who sang as she marched along in a pair of men's boots. She was followed by a crowd of jeering kids. Her speciality was hymn tunes, and sometimes she would stop her singing and call out to the children, "Clear off you little B-----'s," and so on. She was often "run in" for causing a public mischief.

2. Outbreak of war, 1914

On August Bank Holiday, 1914, I went to Yarmouth with several other young men, as this was our custom. But, on this occasion the day was completely ruined by the tense feeling which prevailed. Territorial troops and Reserves were marching to a camp at Caister-on-Sea, and a martial atmosphere pervaded the whole town. When we returned to Thorpe Station, Norwich, there were soldiers on guard with fixed bayonets at all the exits, which tended to make everyone feel most depressed. The atmosphere of war seemed everywhere, and presently Germany invaded Belgium, and we were in it. Our Expeditionary Force was sent out, and was soon in action, but only just escaped annihilation at Mons; it reformed, and, with the French, managed to hold the German advance. The Government called for volunteers, and although most people had the idea that the war would be over in a month, it never looked like that to me.

When the eight of us next met, I said I was joining the army. If any of them decided to do the same, I would meet them at the corner of Rampant Horse St. at 2 p.m. on the 10th August. Only one turned up, and we proceeded to the examination centre in St. Andrew's Hall, and we were told to report at Britannia Barracks on Mousehold on the 22nd of the month where we were to be attested by Major B. W. A. Keppel of Weston Old Hall, near Norwich and became from that time "D" Company of the 8th Battalion the Norfolk Regiment. On that occasion, Sidney Page and I stood in the ranks with a young man who was to be our friend and companion all through the conflict – "Jimmy" Smith. A real "comrade" in good times and bad. We were entrained at Thorpe Station next morning for Shorncliffe Camp in Kent. Arriving there about 4 p.m., we were supplied with a tent for every 12 men. As we were sitting down, someone opened the flap of the tent, and a large tin of plum and apple jam was rolled in, followed by four loaves of bread. This was our ration for the remainder of that day. We were still in our "civvy" clothes, and we wore them until well into November. When it became colder, we had to send home for our overcoats, and we were credited for £1 each for these.

Next morning, after a cup of tea and a biscuit at the Y.M.C.A., we had to fall in for a bathing parade. We marched all the way to Sandgate, a distance of about four miles and enjoyed a swim in the sea. One fellow ran into trouble by losing his false teeth when he was caught off-balance by a large wave. Then we went back to breakfast at camp, and had only our small pocket knives to eat porridge and bacon with. After breakfast, it was platoon drill until 2.30;

lunch at 1 p.m., after which we were taken for a long march and to do some field training. As we had no equipment to carry or rifles, it was quite enjoyable. In the evenings we would go to Folkestone for a show. Luckily we had taken a little money with us, as we were not paid for a month. We had been at Shorncliffe about a month, when Lord Kitchener came to review the troops, but we did not see him as we had no uniforms, and we were taken well away on a kind of exercise-cum-picnic, so that he should not see us in our shabby civilian attire, looking for all the world like some broken-down South American guerrillas. However, the weather was beautiful until it broke late one night with a fearful gale and heavy rain-storm. Our tent pole broke in half, and the wet canvas dropped on the twelve of us. We spent the rest of the night in a large marquee, with a lot of "Old Sweats" who were grumbling about "blinking Rookies" disturbing their night. There must have been some small airships at Dover about this time, we often saw them on the distant skyline, but were unable to get a close view.

In early November we entrained for Colchester, and entered the Meeanee Barracks there; we took over from a regular regiment which had been ordered abroad. Knowing that we were "Rookies," I often wondered if, before the soldiers moved out, they had left a "small" surprise for us. At this time there were fires in the barrack-room; one night, after we were asleep, there was an explosion up the chimney, and the room seemed full of smoke. My friends and I were on some trestles near the chimney, and wondered if the explosion was due to enemy action, but then we found some exploded bullets in the fireplace which must have been left by the former occupants.

Our platoon commander was a nice young man, one Owen Lewis, a nephew of Lord Roberts, but he was the most excitable man I ever met, especially on field days. He was always in trouble with Captain North, our company Commander, as he never completely mastered all the intricacies of military drill on the square or during ceremonial exercises.

* * * * *

Whilst we were at Colchester, we enjoyed ourselves when off duty, which was in the evenings. Our days were fully occupied for His Majesty all the time we were at this military town. Over 20,000 men were living in barracks, hutments and billeted in houses in the area. We spent half our time on manoeuvres in the country round about, taking haversack rations with us, and arriving home about 4 in the afternoon. We were out in the fresh air, and had really enjoyable, but hard, times. Sometimes the Colonel would ask me to hold his horse for him, when he would go to a distant ridge and look at the "enemy" positions through his field glasses. When he returned he would often give me an apple. Colonel Briggs was a nice fatherly old man, and knew just how to treat young soldiers. He was much respected and so was our company commander, Captain North, who, by the way, had a nice daughter much admired by the rank and file. Later, we had to take a firing course on the Middlewick range and were allowed to sit around and smoke until it came to our turn to do the firing. Whilst we were sitting there chatting away, a young officer came along with a squad of men, and seemed unable to get them into the position he had in mind, and was getting hot and bothered. We quietly took the "mickey," and he must have reported it to our captain, who sent our platoon officer along to give us platoon drill until we were wanted on the range; that took the smile off our faces!

On Saturday morning we were always employed on coal fatigue, taking our coal buckets (2 men to a bucket) to the coal yard where first of all, we had to take supplies to our officers' quarters. All the men carrying officers' coal made a point of passing by their own quarters with the coal. A man would be waiting at one of the down-stair windows, and a few large lumps were given to him as the coal-carrier passed by, for later use in the barrack-room stove.

3. Colchester bombed by German aircraft

Whilst we were in the Meeanee Barracks in Colchester, there was an explosion in the night. A German "Taube" aeroplane had dropped the first bomb ever to fall in this country. It caused a direct hit on the Cavalry Barracks, and some soldiers were wounded. After that, there were many raids by "Zeppelins," and a lot of damage was caused in all parts of the country, including London.

When our first uniform was issued to us it consisted of a blue blouse and slacks, with a field service cap. We were almost ashamed to appear in public wearing these awful uniforms. One day we went (Jim, Sid, and I) to London to visit my friend, Ernest, who was an artist with Waterlows the printers. We all went to Lyons' "Corner House" restaurant in Oxford Street, where we had lunch. Whilst there we suffered the final shame of being taken for Belgian refugees!

When we arrived after "lights out" to our barracks that night, and opened the door to enter, a loaf of bread hit us amidships, and this puzzled us, but it transpired that a half pound of margarine had been placed in the bed of one Hugh Palmer, so that when he laid down on it the greasy mess spread all over his blankets.

Hugh was a Norfolk farmer from Kenninghall, and thinking that it was the culprit coming into the room who had committed this outrage, let fly with the loaf. The culprit is rarely found out when he perpetrates a joke on his fellow-men because no-one would give him away.

Sometime after that, Hugh tried to get leave to go home to sort things out for his wife, who was managing the farm in his absence, but was refused permission. So he approached me with a proposition. He would take out a late night pass and go home, and would I kindly hand it in at the guard room when I returned to Barracks? Being of the same build, he said, it shouldn't be difficult if I took care not to show myself too much at the guard room door. He would return on the Sunday night, and no-one would know anything about it. Schemes never turn out as planned, and this was no exception. Early on Sunday morning, we opened up Hugh's bed, and left it unmade. When the orderly sergeant went the rounds, he was told that Palmer had gone to the latrines. He seemed to accept that, but later in the morning he came round again and said, "Palmer back yet?" And we replied, "Not yet!" Then he went into the attack again, employing rather different methods. He said, "We know that Palmer is absent, and also that someone handed his late-night pass in for him. Another thing, we know who he is, so it is up to that man to own up and tell us all he knows before he runs into further trouble." Then the sergeant left again.

Everybody knew that I had handed in the pass, but I was advised to say nothing about it. There was a lot going on, but I just kept silent on the matter, and the act the sergeant had put on was one big bluff. Palmer did not come back on the Sunday night, but arrived about the middle of Monday morning, so he was really for the "high jump." There was a further questioning about the late-night pass which I had handed in, and the whole affair ended, but, of course, Palmer had to appear before the C.O. and explain his action, so he didn't get anything worse than a few days confined to barracks, coupled with fatigue duties after parade, commonly known as "jankers."

* * * * *

Later, we had a forced march to Clacton-on-Sea, about 14 miles from Colchester, and a large number of fellows dropped out, so it was decreed that we must have a lot more "endurance" marches. Our next effort was a march in which the whole 18th Division took part, complete with field kitchens, and the headquarters personnel. Our destination was very "hush-hush" and some of us wondered if, ultimately, we should find ourselves on Southampton Docks, ready to embark for France, but the time was not yet.

At 8 o'clock one morning we marched away with all our equipment, full pack, everything. It was early spring, and quite warm, and it wasn't long before we began to feel really "whacked." But we kept on, with a ten-minute rest each hour, until at about 3 in the afternoon, we found ourselves on the outskirts of Ipswich. When we reached the Woodbridge Road, billeting parties went round the streets commandeering accommodation for a short stay of eight hours. We were due to move off at 11 p.m. that night. The next day we marched to Woodbridge, stayed a few hours there, and then went on (about 27 miles) to a wild desolate place called Hollesley Bay. We stayed there in isolated barns, farm buildings, etc. for a week, during which time extensive divisional manoeuvres took place, night and day. There were no exceptions, everyone had to take part. Sick men had medicine and duty, so everyone really got "sorted out." We slept rough all the time, and the nights were mighty cold, as we had only our great coats to keep us warm.

Then came the journey back, marching along dusty roads, there was no tarmac in those days. Suddenly we would have to leave the road and deploy over adjoining fields to counter an enemy attack. When the enemy retired we would have to form up on the road again, very exhausting work. After we had passed through Woodbridge again we were very tired, and just marched doggedly along without any feeling or interest in anything, but the thought of a good lay-in when we got back to barracks, spurred us on.

* * * * *

In Camp at Codford. When we arrived back at the barracks in Colchester the air was full of rumours – "we were to proceed overseas, we were destined for the Middle East, we were going to India." All proved to be false, as in a few days we were on our way to a camp at Codford in Wiltshire, chalk soil, and very poor hill country. The excess of chalk in the water caused an epidemic of diarrhoea amongst the troops. Then, later, two men from our hut were taken to hospital with meningitis. We thought it was very probable we should get it, and, really were prepared for this to happen. One morning I awoke feeling very queer, with stiffness on each side of my neck; I thought, "this is it!" However, on examination by the doctor, he said, "You have mumps. You will have to be isolated for a fortnight," and I was removed to a bell tent on the edge of a wood, nearly all my meals being left a short distance away for me to fetch. The weather was fine and very warm and, altogether, after the first day, I enjoyed myself, and when I used to wave to my friends marching past with full packs, they used to shake their fists at me. A number of men had very severe attacks, and it transpired an N.C.O., who had been visiting a family in a nearby village, had carried the infection to camp.

It was now so hot that we were issued with shorts and sun flaps for our hats. To make things worse, we spent the rest of the time at Codford in large scale manoeuvres, running and attacking up hill and down, sometimes the exercise taking us as far as Gillingham in Dorsetshire, all very exhausting in the extreme heat. It was quite a common thing for fellows to fall down on their faces from heat and exhaustion.

Then we went on our last leave before going overseas (June 1915) and several were in trouble from overstaying their leave. Afterwards we spent some time on coal fatigue at Warminster Station, coming back looking like sweeps. After a weekend pass to Southampton, my friend found it was only a matter of days before we set sail, and there was great activity everywhere. We all had to have different inoculations (we had already been vaccinated) and were issued with all sorts of different things, and everybody had to be close-cropped.

4. Embarking for France

We went down to Folkestone and boarded ship about midnight. The moon was shining bright, and the journey over was very enjoyable. The sea was calm and we sang to the accompaniment of mouth organs. We also ate some of the cakes which had been sent to us earlier. Arriving at Boulogne at about 2 a.m., we disembarked, and were met by crowds of French civilians going to the quay. Some girls were selling biscuits and oranges. A French sentry on guard over some buildings was leaning on a long rifle in a very casual manner, and I said to my friend, "Jim, I believe we've lost this war." Our destination was a large area called Saint Martin's Plain, and it was full of bell tents. We had to draw bedding and blankets on our arrival, and it was not long after we had settled down that we were itching all over. This was when we had our issue (with the bedding) of "chats" or lice. I would never have thought it possible for a person to become "lousy" in a matter of minutes. Alas, we were never free from them all the time we were in France!

Next day French prostitutes were on the move, and Mounted Military Police were on duty all the time chasing them away from the camp. Another thing that had to be seen to be believed was that Sidney and I were told to

report to the Y. M. C. A. tent for duties, and
found we had to don a white apron, and serve
tea, coffee and cakes, all day. This was O.K.
with us, as we had some jolly exciting meals
whilst we were there.

Then came the journey up the line. We
marched down to Boulogne Station. This was
very different to an English railway station.
Every time a train arrived or departed it seemed
as if all the staff went mad, such excitement,
blowing of whistles and horns, I had never
witnessed the like anywhere before. When we
did get going, we only went short distances, and
then stopped. This happened all the way to
Amiens. Some of the stops were so long one
could get out and buy a bottle of wine, and then,
with a short run, catch the train again. From
Amiens we marched to Molliecourt, where we
had billets in some farm premises. From the
loft above, we could see the town of Albert
with the ruined tower of the cathedral in the
sunshine. It was a beautiful view, and it seemed
such a pity that the place was so knocked about.
Whilst we were at this farm the occupant was
arrested for waving a lighted lantern from the
loft window of his barn, and was marched off by
troops with fixed bayonets. There were quite a
number of traitors arrested from time to time.
When we arrived in the town of Albert we
found the damage far worse than we had

thought. Most of the factory area was completely destroyed. In one place a bicycle and tyre factory had received a direct hit, scattering bicycles and tyres in all directions, and they had just remained so. A fair complete with stalls, sideshows, and swing boats, was standing in an empty space, looking as if it had been functioning when everybody had to leave in a hurry.

Our first time in the line was at La Boisselle, where on our first night, the Jerrys dropped some "coal boxes"* nearby just to celebrate our arrival. The next day one of our number was blown off the firestep by a shell, and was taken away with severe shell-shock; also a young sentry, ignoring advice to "keep his head down," had his brains blown out with an explosive bullet; another fell asleep at his post and was severely reprimanded. All this was due to lack of experience, and, as time went on, one became danger-conscious, and it was almost unheard of for anyone to fall asleep on sentry duty. In this sector of the line we spent many weary months, in and out, with all the monotony of trench warfare, stand-to night and morning, intermittent shell fire, trench mortar fire

---

* "Coal boxes" were named thus on account of the noise they made when exploding, and were sent over by a mine-thrower. The German name was "Minenwerfer."

(Minenwerfer), another Jerry horror weapon, and in the winter the everlasting mud and cold. Some parts of the line were knee-deep in water all winter. Then there was sentry-go on the firestep, two hours on and four off, sapping down the mine shafts, 90 ft. under the ground, with the Royal Engineers. After ten days we would be relieved and go back to the town of Albert, from where we made nightly visits to the line carrying rations and munitions. We even dug gun pits for the artillery.

One of our colleagues, Fred Burton, was asked to form a drum-and-fife band when we were out of the line, and I said to him playfully, "Don't forget me, Fred, when you form your band." I promptly forgot my foolish remark until one day when I was "on-sentry" in the line, a "runner" from Battalion Headquarters arrived and said I was to report immediately to the band sergeant. This really shook me, but I was hoping my small knowledge of music, coupled with a natural aptitude to pick things up quickly, would see me through. I shall never forget the look on "Uncle J's" face the first time he saw me marching down the French village street, "playing" an F flute. As I approached he just put his hand over his eyes and shook with laughing. Later, I had to call on my natural ability still further, when they formed a brass band, and I was presented with a "flugel horn" – an instrument which added ...

tone and mellowness to the cornets
(I hope)! There were compensations
in being a bandsman, one was
excused duties in the line at
first, so that we could put in
a lot of practice and become
proficient, especially myself,
who had never played an
instrument of any kind. My
only saving grace was the
fact that I had some knowledge of music, especially as it
was found that no band music
had been sent, for my instrument and I had to write my
own, which was passed by the
bandmaster as being ok, to
my great relief. Whilst we were
practising, the soldiers near our
building, have often said if
we didn't watch it, they would
shoot us (in fun, of course).
    When proficient, we were all
trained as battalion bombers
in readiness for a big attack
which was one of the rumours
in the battalion, just then...

The text in the diaries up to this point has consisted of pasted-in copies of typeset material. The diaries now continue in manuscript, with facing transcription.

... tone and mellowness to the cornets (I hope!) There were compensations in being a bandsman, one was excused duties in the line at first, so that, we could put in a lot of practice and become proficient, especially myself, who had never played an instrument of any kind. My only saving grace was the fact that I had some knowledge of music, especially as it was found that no band music had been sent, for my instrument and I had to write my own, which was passed by the bandmaster as being OK, to my great relief. Whilst we were practising, the soldiers near our building have often said if we didn't watch it, they would shoot us (in fun of course).

When proficient we were all trained as battalion bombers in readiness for a big attack which was one of the rumours in the battalion, just then...

"Ten Days' Leave

During the war 1914-1918, a small
number of soldiers, serving in
France, would be given leave
to go to "Blighty" for ten days.
Names were drawn out of a
box and the lucky people were
given 300 Francs from their
"credits" and, together with
others from the Division would
go home by boat and the ten
days would form a nice break
from the monotony of trench
warfare.

The music-halls came up with
a "catchy" song about this leave,
as follows:

It's a fine time for a soldier,
 When he's home on his ten days
  leave;
He sees his Aunt Maria,
He sees his Uncle Jim;
He tells you what the General
  said,
And what he said to him."

[Repeat first two lines] ...

5. Ten days' leave, Feb 1916

During the war 1914-1918, a small number of soldiers serving in France would be given leave to go to "Blighty" for ten days. Names were drawn out of a box and the lucky people were given 300 francs from their "credits" and, together with others from the Division, would go home by boat and the ten days would form a nice break from the monotony of trench warfare.

The music-halls came up with a "catchy" song about this leave as follows:

> "It's a fine time for a soldier,
> When he's home on his ten days' leave;
> He sees his Aunt Maria,
> He sees his Uncle Jim;
> He tells you what the General said,
> And what he said to him."
> [Repeat first two lines...]

I came home with a leave party in February, 1916, there were about 50 of us in charge of a sergeant and, as we marched out of the village, the French people were out in the street, calling out "Bon Permission". It was quite an "occasion".

Boarding a train at Amiens, we were able to buy a luncheon basket for five francs (3s. 4d.), which contained half a chicken, a long loaf of bread, some unsalted butter, a jar of jam, and a bottle of red wine.

When we reached the docks at Le Havre, everyone was "frisked" for souvenirs as it was not allowed by the Army, mainly because there had been accidents from shell cases which still had explosive material in them.

As soon as we were out at sea, almost all were seasick. It was a very rough passage and everyone was most thankful when we arrived at Southampton.

After being checked again at the docks, we were put on the leave train...

Ten days' leave, Feb 1916

I came home with a leave party in February 1916, there were about 50 of us in charge of a sergeant and, as we marched out of the village, the French people were out in the street, calling out "Bon[ne] permission!" It was quite an "occasion."

Boarding a train at Amiens, we were able to buy a luncheon basket for five francs (3s.7d.), which contained half a chicken, a long loaf of bread, some unsalted butter, a jar of jam, and a bottle of red wine.

When we reached the docks at Le Havre, everyone was "frisked" for souvenirs as it was not allowed by the army, mainly because there had been accidents from shell cases which still had explosive material in them.

As soon as we were out at sea almost all were seasick. It was a very rough passage and everyone was most thankful when we arrived at Southampton.

After being checked again at the docks, we were put on the leave train ...

to London. During the journey.
one of the soldiers in our carriage, surprised us all by standing up and withdrawing a long,
finely engraved cavalry sword.
from the leg of his trousers. How
the military police overlooked
this large weapon is a miracle.

By the time we reached London,
we were all famished after the
channel crossing and made for
one of Lyon's cafés. and ordered
some stewed steak and boiled
potatoes. The waitress just smiled
and said: "We have nothing but
vegetable pie, so we ordered two
each and for sweets we had
boiled rice. Not at all the sort
of meal, we had been thinking
of. and easily the worst meal
we had eaten since joining up
in 1914.

A number of us boarded the
Norwich train., which stopped
at every station; we kept looking at the familiar names, but
as darkness came on, a dense
fog settled down, and although
all the station lamps were lit,
we were unable to see...

to London. During the journey one of the soldiers in our carriage surprised us all by standing up and withdrawing a long, finely engraved cavalry sword from the leg of his trousers. How the military police overlooked this large weapon is a miracle.

By the time we reached London, we were all famished after the Channel crossing and made for one of the Lyons cafés, and ordered some stewed steak and boiled potatoes. The waitress just smiled and said: "We have nothing but vegetable pie," so we ordered two each and for sweets we had boiled rice. Not at all the sort of meal we had been thinking of and easily the worst meal we had eaten since joining up in 1914.

A number of us boarded the Norwich train, which stopped at every station; we kept looking at the familiar names, but as darkness came on, a dense fog settled down, and although all the station lamps were lit, we were unable to see…

the names, so, finally, we had no idea where we were as the train often stopped away from any station, however, when we arrived at the next station we heard someone on the platform shout in broad Norfolk dialect: "Ha yer sin thet owd dawg inybhe, Joe?"

Never, were we more relieved to know that, at least, we were now in Norfolk. I had to get off the train at Diss, faced with the prospect of a 1½ mile walk to my home in a dense fog. After leaving the main road, I had to follow a footpath over a large heath and then a narrow road with tall hedges each side.

I was nearly home now and, picturing the surprise on his face when I turned up. Next moment I was thrown to the ground after falling over a soldier's legs lying across the path. His head being in the hedge.

He was dead drunk, and after I had got him on to his feet, he could not stand, and after striking me...

the names, so, finally, we had no idea where we were as the train often stopped away from any station, however, when we arrived at the next station we heard someone on the platform shout in broad Norfolk dialect: "Ha yer sin thet owd dawg inywhe, Joe?"

Never were we more relieved to know that, at least, we were now in Norfolk. I had to get off the train at Diss, faced with the prospect of a 1½ mile walk to my home in a dense fog. After leaving the main road, I had to follow a footpath over a large heath and then a narrow road with tall hedges each side.

I was nearly home now and picturing the surprise on his face when I turned up. Next moment I was thrown to the ground after falling over a soldier's legs lying across the path. His head being in the hedge.

He was dead drunk, and after I had got him to his feet, he could not stand, and after striking me...

a glancing blow, he crashed
to the ground again. I could do
nothing to help him and had
to leave him there.

My father and sister were so
surprised to see me and soon
were able to dish up a good
dinner – and I was ready for it.

Next day, my sister arranged
to hire a horse and trap and
drive over to Pulham to see
some old family friends. My
sister's friend driving. Just
the three of us.

I was not very happy at the
way the horse was behaving –
it had a curious habit of stopping when another vehicle was
approaching us and backing.
Sure enough, when we were walking the horse up a hill and had
just reached the corner, a Royal
Navy Air Service lorry came
round at speed cutting it rather
fine, and swerving to avoid our
vehicle, caught us a glancing
blow and swung the cart round
on its axle;

No-one was hurt, but the cart
was damaged...

a glancing blow, he crashed to the ground again. I could do nothing to help him and had to leave him there.

My father and sister were so surprised to see me and soon were able to dish up a good dinner – and I was ready for it.

Next day, my sister arranged to hire a horse and trap and drive over to Pulham to see some old family friends, my sister's friend driving. Just the three of us.

I was not very happy at the way the horse was behaving – it had a curious habit of stopping when another vehicle was approaching us and backing. Sure enough, when we were walking the horse up a hill and had just reached the corner, a Royal Navy Air Service lorry came round at speed cutting it rather fine, and swerving to avoid our vehicle, caught us a glancing blow and swung the cart round on its axle.

No-one was hurt, but the cart was damaged...

and we had to take the pony
out, my sister leading this most
unpredictable animal, whilst I
had to pull the cart into Pulham
where I had to leave it for repairs.
  The horse was stabled for the
night and we all went to our
friends to tea. Later, in the
evening, we had to get back
to Diss by rail. Altogether, this
little "spree" cost us almost £4.

          ×   ×   ×   ×

  Next day, I journeyed to Norwich
by train to see my girl friend
and, before we had gone very
far, it started to snow and
kept that way all the rest of
the holiday. Snow was quite
deep in Norwich which kept us
indoors quite a lot; however,
we went to a few shows, also
spent some evenings with old
friends.
  Then I had to say good-bye to
my girl friend and went home
again, to spend the end of the
time with my father... Then the
journey to London and Southampton, where we were to take
          the boat back to France
                              ...

and we had to take the pony out, my sister leading this most unpredictable animal, whilst I had to pull the cart into Pulham where I had to leave it for repairs.

The horse was stabled for the night and we all went to our friends to tea. Later, in the evening, we had to get back to Diss by rail. Altogether this little "spree" cost us almost £4.

* * * * *

Next day, I journeyed to Norwich by train to see my girl friend and, before we had gone very far, it started to snow and kept that way all the rest of the holiday. Snow was quite deep in Norwich which kept us indoors quite a lot; however, we went to a few shows, also spent some evenings with old friends.

Then I had to say goodbye to my girl friend and went home again, to spend the end of the time with my father…. Then the journey to London and Southampton, where we were to take the boat back to France…

It was now snowing heavily again, accompanied by severe gales so we had to spend the night in some draughty sheds at the docks; next morning we went on board the steamer and went as far as Southampton "roads", when we were ordered to return to the docks again as the sea was too rough for us to proceed.

We spent two more days at the docks, before being given the order to get on board again; there didn't seem much difference in the force of the gale, but we did manage to get away this time.

When we had got clear of the "Roads", the sea was very rough, and I was placed on deck on submarine duty.

I doubt very much if a submarine would have ventured out in those awful waves, which took the ship on the crest and then plunged down, down, down.

Many times up on deck, I had an awful feeling that the ship would never last the journey, I had to put my arm through an iron...

Ten days' leave, Feb 1916

It was now snowing heavily again, accompanied by severe gales, so we had to spend the night in some draughty sheds at the docks; next morning we went on board the steamer and went as far as Southampton "roads," when we were ordered to return to the docks again as the sea was too rough for us to proceed.

We spent two more days at the docks, before being given the order to get on board again; there didn't seem much difference in the force of the gale, but we did manage to get away this time.

When we had got clear of the "Roads," the sea was very rough and I was placed on deck on submarine duty.

I doubt very much if a submarine would have ventured out in those awful waves, which took the ship on the crest and then plunged down, down, down.

Many times up on deck I had an awful feeling that the ship would never last the journey. I had to put my arm though an iron...

stanchion to stop being washed overboard. I was never relieved from my duty on deck, but went below to find the sergeant and find out why I had been left for hours without "relief".

I was blandly told that "they" were not bothering about the submarine duty any more as it far too rough for them to be out. However, I was given some hot drink — and did I need it!

We started off for Le Havre, but had to "hug" the coast most of the time and eventually saw the cliffs of Boulogne. It had taken us 14 hours to get this port — and it was just getting daylight

The two drunken Scotchmen who were so drunk they had to be carried aboard at Southampton, were the luckiest people on the voyage. They didn't know a thing about the awful voyage and the danger we were in.

I was now going back to the war area, but I have never felt so scared as I had been on that wretched ship...

stanchion to stop being washed overboard. I was never relieved from my duty on deck, but went below to find the sergeant and find out why I had been left for hours without "relief."

I was blandly told that they were not bothering about the submarine duty any more as it was far too rough for them to be out. However, I was given some hot drink – and did I need it!

We started off for Le Havre, but had to "hug" the coast most of the time and eventually saw the cliffs at Boulogne. It had taken us 14 hours to get to this port – and it was just getting daylight.

The two drunken Scotchmen, who were so drunk they had to be carried aboard at Southampton, were the luckiest people on the voyage. They didn't know a thing about the awful voyage and the danger we were in.

I was now going back to the war area, but I had never felt so scared as I had been on that wretched ship...

This page and the following short chapter are in typeset paste-up in the diaries.

When the leave party arrived back, the Battalion were on rest at Etinheim, near Bray-sur-Somme, and this was a very nice little village where the people and troops got on very well together. It was while we were at this place that we had to take over a sector of the front line at a place called Maricourt. Here the line was only about 20 yards from Jerry's, and one had to be very careful not to expose oneself. One good thing, we did not get much shell fire in the front line because of the closeness, but mortar fire and hand grenades were frequent. When we were relieved we only returned to some more trenches (reserve) about 300 yards away.

However, we were only there for a few days, when we were told we were going back to a small village the other side of Amiens. There were a lot of rumours current, but nothing authentic about our "rest" behind the lines.

6. Preparing for first of July

It was a long march to Amiens, but I shall never forget the welcome we received. The whole population were lining the streets and, when our band started to play a gay tune, the excitement of these French people overflowed and everyone mingled with troops and we were presented with apples and pears and managed to take a quick drink of wine in our passage through the city. It was a wonderful experience.

The small village which was to be our "home" for about two months was a most picturesque little place and we all "took to it" at once. On arrival, we had a short talk by the Colonel and it was then that we were told we were to have a long period of intensive field training, during which our tactics would consist, mostly, of Open Warfare, as opposed to trench warfare. It was lovely May weather and, though the training was arduous, it was much enjoyed. We also had the luxury of a hot bath now and then.

After a long spell of trench warfare, with its monotonous and dreary routine and continuous day-to-day casualties, this small village was *heaven*. About the middle of June, replacements of men from England started to arrive. This in turn gave rise to all sorts of rumours which were, according to military parlance, "straight from the horse's mouth" – the Colonel told his horse, the horse told the groom and he passed the news on to us. A very simple procedure.

After this training, we marched to a small town in the battle area called Bray-sur-Somme; here the military activity was on a scale never before seen by our Division. There were French, Indian and British, combined with Colonial troops from both countries. We realised a big battle was imminent. A day or two later a terrific bombardment of the German lines began and continued for a fortnight. Things were very rough, with the German retaliatory artillery fire going on all the time. The noise was deafening.

We were now digging assembly trenches and suffered many casualties during this operation, but "the show" had to go on. We were now told that the first of July was "the day," and on the morning of the "first" about 5 a.m., troops were on the move everywhere and by 6.30 a.m., we were in the assembly trenches. Everything was very tense and one kept hearing remarks such as: "We're only here for life!" and "How long is duration?"

Summary of Somme Battles

The first battle of the Somme was launched to relieve the pressure of the German offensive in the Verdun sector, held by the French, and took the form of a series of attacks over a wide front on fortified villages, woods and redoubts, or strong points.

The advance began on the 1st of July, 1916, with 14 days preliminary bombardment.

The British captured Fricourt, Mametz and Montauban; whilst the French had reached and secured Biaches. Then, after desperate struggles, the British captured Trones and Mametz woods.

On the 14th of July came the battle for Delville Wood, which changed hands many times before being finally secured by the end of July, 1916; then the village of Longueval was captured and held.

The fighting was of a terrible character, owing to the strength of the enemy positions and
counter-attacks
. . .

7. Summary of Somme battles

The first battle of the Somme was launched to relieve the pressure of the German offensive in the Verdun sector, held by the French and took the form of a series of attacks over a wide front on fortified villages, woods and redoubts, or strong points.

The advance began on the 1st of July, 1916, with 14 days preliminary bombardment.

The British captured Fricourt, Mametz and Montaubon; whilst the French had reached and secured Biaches. Then, after desperate struggles, the British captured Trones and Mametz woods.

On the 14th of July came the battle for Delville Wood, which changed hands many times before being finally secured by the end of July 1916; then the village of Longueval was captured and held.

The fighting was of a terrible character, owing to the strength of the enemy positions and counter-attacks…

During August, the French and British had reached the outskirts of Cléry and Peronne.

Guillemont was taken on September 3rd, 1916 and, in another great attack on the 15th of the month, from Martin-puich to the Somme, tanks were used for the first time.

These were not popular with the infantry, as each tank had to take a number of them with it as "guards", as the tanks attracted the artillery fire of the enemy. There was, of course, a certain element of surprise to the Germans.

During the next few weeks, Thiepval, Guedecourt, Marval and Combles were taken; also the Zollern redoubts were captured on October 3rd.

Counter-attacks by the enemy were numerous and costly to both sides.

Following this were strong British attacks on the River Ancre front. In these two battles the British losses were 22,923 officers and

During August, the French and British had reached the outskirts of Cléry and Peronne.

Guillemont was taken on September 3rd, 1916 and, in another great attack on the 15th of the month, from Martinpuich to the Somme, tanks were used for the first time.

These were not popular with the infantry, as each tank had to take a number of them with it as "guards", as the tanks attracted the artillery fire of the enemy. There was of course, a certain element of surprise to the Germans.

During the next few weeks, Thiepval, Guedecourt, Marual and Combles were taken; also the Lollern redoubts were captured on October 3rd.

Counter-attacks by the enemy were numerous and costly to both sides.

Following this were strong British attacks on the River Ancre front. In these two battles the British losses were 22,923 officers and...

476,553

men. (An officers life in those days was averaged at 14 days).

A frightful price to pay for such small gains

Owing to the collapse of the Russian "steamroller" in 1917, the Germans were able to withdraw all their best troops from the Russian front to the Western front, until they √1½ had million men, with over 16,000 guns.

* On March 21st, 1918, they captured in a great offensive all the ground lost during the Somme battles, carrying their line forward to within a few miles of the Cathedral city of Amiens

x x x x

In course of time, however, the entry of America, with all their vast resources of men and guns, was the turning point of the war.

* on the Cambrai front.

54

476,553 men. (An officer's life in those days was averaged at 14 days).

A frightful price to pay for such small gains.

Owing to the collapse of the Russian "steamroller" in 1917, the Germans were able to withdraw all their best troops from the Russian front to the Western Front, until they had 1½ million men, with over 16,000 guns.

*On March 21st, 1918, they captured in a great offensive all the ground lost during the Somme battles, carrying their line forward to within a few miles of the Cathedral city of Amiens.

* * * * *

In course of time, however, the entry of America, with all their vast resources of men and guns, was the turning point of the war.

*on the Cambrai front.

Trench Raid

Prior to the 1st of July, 1916

On or about the 28th of June, 1916, information was required by the Battalion commander as to how strong, if at all, the German front line was held; also information as to the name of the unit holding the line, stressing that it would be very desirable if a prisoner could be brought back when they returned.

The time arranged for the raid was 2 a.m., a time when it is well-nigh impossible to identify objects in no-man's land with any certainty.

It was arranged that the shelling of the German front line would be advanced by 300 yards, so that the shells would be going over our heads, but exploding farther away. This would help to keep the enemy's heads down; whilst we were going there and coming back. It had to be a hit-and-run affair. Six of us from the Battalion bombers

56

8. Trench raid prior to the 1ˢᵗ July, 1916

On or about the 28ᵗʰ of June 1916, information was required by the Battalion commander as to how strong[ly], if at all, the German front line was held; also information as to the name of the unit holding the line, stressing that it would be very desirable if a prisoner could be brought back when they returned.

The time arranged for the raid was 2 a.m., a time when it is well-nigh impossible to identify objects in no-man's land with any certainty.

It was arranged that the shelling of the German front line would be advanced by 300 yards, so that the shells would be going over our heads, but exploding farther away. This would help to keep the enemy's heads down; whilst we were going there and coming back. It had to be a hit and run affair. Six of us from the Battalion bombers...

were chosen for this operation,
all men with experience of
attack and defence in different
parts of the line.

First we all had our faces
blacked, then we discarded our
steel hats and wore "balaclava"
helmets (a woollen head gear) instead. Then, armed with a stout,
wooden club, studded with horse
shoe nails, two "Mills" bombs per
man, together with side arms,,
we were briefed for the "show":

"Make your way quietly out
of the trenches, creeping slowly
towards the enemy lines, taking
care not to get your feet entangled
in any odd wire lying about.
"Freeze" every time a light goes
up, watch for signals from your
corporal, as no words will be
spoken.

"Wait a short distance from
the "Jerry" trenches and watch
for a sentry to 'pop' his head up
for a quick look', at the same
time cutting a passage through
the wire. Two men to move
close to the ...

were chosen for this operation, all men with experience of attack and defence in different parts of the line.

First we all had our faces blacked, then we discarded our steel hats and wore "balaclava" helmets (a woollen head gear) instead. Then, armed with a stout wooden club, studded with horse shoe nails, two "Mills" bombs per man, together with side arms, we were briefed for the "show."

"Make your way quietly out of the trenches, creeping slowly towards the enemy lines, taking care not to get your feet entangled in any odd wire lying about.

"Freeze every time a light goes up, watch for signals from your corporal, as no words will be spoken.

"Wait a short distance from the 'Jerry' trenches and watch for a sentry to 'pop' his head up for a quick look, at the same time cutting a passage through the wire. Two men to move close to the...

the German parapet. Remainder
will act as "cover" in case anything goes wrong, (in this event,
the party will have to make a
hurried retreat.)

"Each man, from this time will
have to act on his own initiative,
keeping a sharp look-out for
any signals from your corporal;
also watch for any activity in
'Jerry' trenches whilst action is
proceeding."

So we all crept silently out of
our trenches, through a passage
previously made through our
own wire, and soon were out
in no-man's land, feeling as
conspicuous as a double-decker
bus. Intermittent rifle and
machine-gun fire was going on
all the time, coupled with with
"lights" from both sides.

We felt we must be seen, but
were lucky and reached a spot
where we watched for a sentry
to take a quick look round, but
not a sign of movement anywhere.
We became uneasy
...

60

German parapet. Remainder will act as "cover" in case anything goes wrong (in this event, the party will have to make a hurried retreat).

"Each man, from this time will have to act on his own initiative, keeping a sharp look-out for any signals from your corporal; also watch for any activity in 'Jerry' trenches whilst action is proceeding."

So we all crept silently out of our trenches, through a passage previously made through our own wire, and soon were out in no-man's land, feeling as conspicuous as a double-decker bus. Intermittent rifle and machine-gun fire was going on all the time, coupled with "lights" from both sides.

We felt we <u>must</u> be seen, but were lucky and reached a spot where we watched for a sentry to take a quick look round, but not a sign of movement anywhere. We became uneasy…

Things were not going according to plan, so the Corporal "prodded" two of us and motioned us to go forward.

We were all very tense, as we approached the enemy front line and were expecting a challenge or a burst of fire at any moment, but nothing happened, so we leaned over the parapet to take a quick look in the trench.

Not a sign of life anywhere, the trench was practically full of earth and it appeared obvious that all German troops, had moved out to their support lines, so we crept back and joined the corporal and the rest of the party.

He motioned that we were to return to our own lines, and we were anxious to get back, as the operation had already taken longer than we had planned.

In addition, we didn't want to be caught in our own artillery barrage, when it came down on the enemy front line again. The journey back was...

Trench raid prior to the 1st July, 1916

Things were not going according to plan, so the Corporal "prodded" two of us and motioned us to go forward.

We were all very tense, as we approached the enemy front line and were expecting a challenge or a burst of fire at any moment, but nothing happened so we leaned over the parapet to take a quick look in the trench.

Not a sign of life anywhere, the trench was practically full of earth and it appeared obvious that all German troops had moved out to their support lines, so we crept back and joined the corporal and the rest of the party.

He motioned that we were to return to our own lines, and we were anxious to get back as the operation had already taken longer than we had planned.

In addition, we didn't want to be caught in our own artillery barrage, when it came down on the enemy front line again. The journey back was...

uneventful, except for an increase
in enemy shell fire; it took us
longer too, having to take
evasive action more frequently.
but, eventually reached our own
lines, safely, feeling that the
whole action. was a "wash-out."

However, the Corporal reported
everything we had seen and
all that happened throughout
the operation, and he told us
afterwards that the Colonel
had seemed very satisfied
such information as we had
brought back. Anyway, we
were lucky to get back without
any casualties. No other raids
were made before the 1st July.

In conclusion, it is a fallacy
to suppose that shell fire splits
up barbed wire. We found that
in spite of all our artillery fire.
it was not broken up, but
mixed up and entangled in
such a way as to present a
more effective obstacle: We found
this out when making a passage
through the enemy
wire.

uneventful, except for an increase in enemy shell fire; it took us longer too, having to take evasive action more frequently, but eventually reached our own lines, safely, feeling that the whole action was a "wash-out."

* * * * *

However, the Corporal reported everything we had seen and all that happened throughout the operation, and he told us afterwards that the Colonel had seemed very satisfied [with] such information as we had brought back. Anyway, we were lucky to get back without any casualties. No other raids were made before the 1ˢᵗ July.

* * * * *

In conclusion, it is a fallacy to suppose that shell fire splits up barbed wire. We found that in spite of all our artillery fire, it was not broken up, but mixed up and entangled in such a way as to present a more effective obstacle: We found this out when making a passage through the enemy wire.

9. The attack*

Then came the order to "go over." Everything had been planned, but things did not go according to plan – mines timed to blow-up one minute before our troops went over the top, did not explode until our men were on the top of the mined area so that numerous men were killed and wounded before the advance really began.

We were in the bombers and the last to go over, so we missed this holocaust. Our job was to "winkle-out" Jerrys who were still sheltering in the dug-outs. They were reluctant to come out, having been told that the British shot all German prisoners. This was entirely wrong, of course, so we often had to call to them and threaten to throw a bomb down if they didn't come out. I cannot remember having any food all day; only water now and then.

One Jerry strong point held out against many

Chapters 9 and 10 are in pasted-up typeset text in the diaries.

attacks, but eventually, we had to send for a Stokes gun battery which soon brought them out with their hands up. Next followed a great tragedy, "Montaubon Abbey" a strongly fortified German trench, refused to surrender and the commander of our troops sent a message back asking for artillery support, but no response came from the artillery, so a final onslaught was made and the trench taken. Almost at the moment of occupation by our troops, our artillery put down a devastating "barrage" on the trench, causing havoc amongst those who had just taken it.

We spent the rest of the day as carrying parties for the advancing troops and lost a large number of men, killed and wounded, in passing along a sunken road, which was continually strafed by German shell fire. Coming back from one of these excursions I must have taken a wrong turning in the "maze" of trenches and completely lost my way. Time after time I passed the same two dead bodies lying in the trench.

It had been a hard day, without food, and I suddenly felt exhausted, having walked many miles trying to find a way out. It was now quite dark and impossible to find ones way over the top, so I sat down and waited, hoping someone would come along. Finally, a young officer in the "Suffolks" came along with two men and they directed me back to my base.

My friends were all very relieved to see me, thinking I must have "stopped one." They were in the middle of a welcome meal and I very heartily joined them.

10. Re-taking Delville Wood

Next day, our relief arrived and our unit went back for a rest to Bray-sur-Somme for a few days. Two or three days later we had to go back and retake Delville Wood which the Jerrys had recaptured. After a briefing, we went over the top at 6.30 a.m., having to climb over a large number of dead bodies to advance.

The Corporal and Sergeant were killed at the moment of entry into the wood, the victims of some Jerry snipers in the treetops. They were soon brought down and we advanced in the face of heavy fire from artillery and small arms. As we approached the opposite side of the wood, two German soldiers came towards us with their hands up. One was a mere boy of 18; the other was a big red-haired soldier, whose appearance may have rather frightened one of our younger soldiers who, without any hesitation, started to fire at them. I shouted to him to stop and told him what I thought of his actions.

At the same time I ran to the German prisoners and found the young man severely wounded in the wrist. Binding up his wound, he kept saying "Kamerad" to me all the while. I was suddenly conscious that all rifle fire had ceased, and wondered if it was just coincidence, or a sporting gesture by the enemy. Pressing on to the edge of the wood, we tried to dig ourselves in, but there were too many tree roots and no other cover at all, so we were in a very exposed position, holding on, as we had been told reinforcements would arrive. None ever did, until by 6 p.m., there were just two of us left out of seventy men. We were faint and hungry and thought we would have some food (biscuits and cheese) from our haversacks. That was the last thing we ever did in that situation. A sniper blew my companion's brains out and I had a bullet through my nose. On my way back (alone), four of our men, thinking I was a Jerry in British uniform, told me to put my rifle down, but I refused and told them what I thought of them. On to the dressing station and six miles down the sunken road to the hospital, where I arrived in an exhausted condition, having drunk the whole of the contents of my two water bottles to keep myself going. This sunken road was littered with the dead and dying; casualties from the devastating artillery fire of the Germans.

Re-taking Delville Wood

I had more than a dozen near-misses on the way down. One, dropped not more than a yard away and I was just waiting for the explosion, when I suddenly realised it was a dud. I saw our divisional chaplain who was walking beside a party of stretcher-bearers, when a big shell landed in their midst and all were killed. I passed them on my way down.

In the distance one saw men walking down this sunken road when, suddenly there would be a shell burst, with a lot of smoke and, when this cleared they would have disappeared. Eventually, I reached the field hospital, where I fainted off. Later, some of us were taken to the railway station to be put on a hospital train. This was bombed on our arrival and we had to take cover. After some delay the train started off.

How sweet it seemed to hear the rhythmic movement of the train, putting more and more distance between us and "the hell" we had just left. All we could think of was a rest in a comfortable bed and time to forget.

I have never been able to completely do this and dream of the sunken road to this day.

1916

In Hospital at Rouen (France)

This was the hospital where all the badly-wounded men were being cared for. Some were so badly-disfigured that they had to stay in this hospital until they had been given some plastic surgery or similar treatment. Eventually, they would go to the hospital for badly-wounded soldiers at Roehampton in England, where some would have to remain for a long time.

The slightly-wounded men were only at Rouen until a hospital ship arrived to take them to "blighty." I was classified as "walking wounded" because the wounds in my face and nose required special treatment. All they did was to change the dressings each day. But after some days, I began to have "blinding" pains in the head

Then, one day we were marched down to the quay to be taken on board the hospital ship "Scythia." Arriving there about 10 a.m. we had to watch all the stretcher cases

. . .

11. In hospital at Rouen, 1916

This was the hospital where all the badly-wounded men were being cared for. Some were so badly disfigured that they had to stay in this hospital until they had been given some plastic surgery or similar treatment. Eventually they would go to the hospital for badly-wounded soldiers at Roehampton in England, where some would have to remain for a long time.

The slightly-wounded men were only at Rouen until a hospital ship arrived to taken them to "blighty." I was classified as "walking" wounded because the wounds in my face and nose required special treatment. All they did was to change the dressings each day. But after some days, I began to have "blinding" pains in the head.

Then, one day we were marched down to the quay to be taken on board the hospital ship "Scythia." Arriving there about 10 a.m., we had to watch all the stretcher cases...

being carried on to the vessel.
It was July and very hot for
people with head wounds to
stand there in sun. At midday, nurses of the British Red
Cross brought us some tea and
biscuits, so we all sat down
and enjoyed the refreshing
quality of the tea; then during
the afternoon, my head started
to throb and I can remember
saying to the man who sat next
to me "I do feel queer". Then I
must have fainted, because when
I came round, I was lying in
bed, so surmised I must have
been carried on board, when
I "passed out".

To my great surprise, it was
now morning and, after breakfast I was taken to the top deck
by "lift", where an hospital sister
syringed and cleaned up my
wounds for the first time since
I had left Delville Wood (Somme).
Feeling very much better, I was
able to enjoy the trip over the
Channel to Southampton. The
ship was heavily camouflaged

being carried on to the vessel. It was July and very hot for people with head wounds to stand there in sun. At midday, nurses of the British Red Cross brought us some tea and biscuits, so we all sat down and enjoyed the refreshing quality of the tea; then during the afternoon, my head started to throb and I can remember saying to the man who sat next to me "I do feel queer." Then I must have fainted because when I came round, I was lying in bed, so surmised I must have been carried on board, when I "passed out."

To my great surprise, it was now morning and after breakfast I was taken to the top deck by "lift" where a hospital sister syringed and cleaned up my wounds for the first time since I had left Delville Wood (Somme). Feeling very much better, I was able to enjoy the trip over the channel to Southampton. The ship was heavily camouflaged.

Disembarking at about 10.30 a.m., the Red Cross people escorted us to the hospital train.

When we were all comfortably seated, R.A.M.C. men came along with a book, asking each one of us the name of our home towns, so that they could arrange for us to be sent to a hospital as near as possible to our home town. I gave them "Norwich in Norfolk" but where I eventually arrived at West Didsbury, near Manchester, I lost all faith in this particular organisation.

. There were hundreds of men in this former Infirmary at West Didsbury - British, Australian and New Zealand and, to my great and agreeable surprise, two men with whom I had joined up with in 1914. We had some very nice evenings out, local families asking us to spend an evening with them.

This was an ideal situation, until one morning a number of Canadians stood up and said "their eggs were bad." The

Disembarking at about 10.30 a.m., the Red Cross people escorted us to the hospital train.

When we were all comfortably seated, R.A.M.C. men came along with a book, asking each one of us the name of our home towns, so that they could arrange for us to be sent to a hospital as near as possible to our home town. I gave them "Norwich in Norfolk", but where I eventually arrived at West Didsbury, near Manchester, I lost all faith in this particular organisation.

There were hundreds of men in this former Infirmary at West Didsbury – British, Australian, and New Zealand and, to my great and agreeable surprise, two men with whom I had joined up with in 1914. We had some very nice evenings out, local families asking us to spend an evening with them.

This was an ideal situation, until, one morning a number of Canadians stood up and said "their eggs were bad." The

Doctor was a pompous type of man, with very little tact, not at all the kind of man to deal with a crowd of high-spirited Colonials. He adopted the attitude that the eggs were all fresh eggs, delivered from a local farm only the day previous and that in his opinion they were making a frivolous complaint.

One soldier took his egg up to the rostrum where the doctor was standing and asked him to examine and smell the egg, but he refused to examine it, or even look at it.

At this refusal, all the Colonials stood up and then walked out of the dining hall. The doctor ordered them to return, but the Colonials just carried on and left the room.

The doctor was furious and told those still in their seats that all evening passes out would be cancelled and no-one would be allowed out of the hospital grounds.

This statement had the effect

Doctor was a pompous type of man, with very little tact, not at all the kind of man to deal with a crowd of high spirited Colonials. He adopted the attitude that the eggs were all fresh eggs, delivered from a local farm only the day previous and, that in his opinion they were making a frivolous complaint.

One soldier took his egg up to the rostrum where the doctor was standing and asked him to examine and smell the egg, but he refused to examine it or even look at it.

At this refusal, all the Colonials stood up and then walked out of the dining hall. The doctor ordered them to return but the Colonials just carried on and left the room.

The doctor was furious and told those still in their seats that all evening passes out would be cancelled and no-one would be allowed out of the hospital grounds.

This statement had the effect

of a red rag to a bull, and their
reaction was a determination
to go out for the evening and
defy the doctor's order. The main
entrance gates were locked, but
it was found that near the
high wall which surrounded
the rear gardens of the hospital,
there were trees, easily climable,
by which one could get out of
the gardens.

I think almost everyone must
have slipped up one or other
of these "conveniently-placed trees
and enjoyed a night out as they
had before the "egg" incident;
now, the troops were arriving
back in twos and threes, until
the crowd outside resembled
a football occasion.

The big gates were locked, with
the doctor and porter (poor man)
waiting to take all our names
as we made our way, one at a
time through the small gate at
the side. That is "what the
doctor had ordered", but little
did he know of the men with
whom he was dealing. As
soon as

of a red rag to a bull, and their reaction was a determination to go out for the evening and defy the doctor's order. The main entrance gates were locked but it was found that near the high wall which surrounded the rear gardens of the hospital there were trees easily climbable by which one could get out of the gardens.

I think almost everyone must have slipped up one or other of these conveniently placed trees and enjoyed a night out as they had before the "egg" incident; now, the troops were arriving back in twos and threes until the crowd outside resembled a football occasion.

The big gates were locked, with the doctor and porter (poor man) waiting to take all our names as we made our way, one at a time through the small gate at the side. That is "what the doctor had ordered," but little did he know of the men with whom he was dealing. As soon as

that small gate was opened,
a crowd of laughing soldiers
forced their way through, taking
the doctor and porter with them,
dashing straight to wards
where they were sleeping.

I suddenly remembered a
back staircase (it could have
been a fire escape) and used this
for a quick entry to my ward,
and hopped straight into bed,
fully clothed and feigned
sleep, just as the doctor and the
sister came to inspect the "sleepers".
All appeared sound asleep. It
was dark and we got away
with it, but not quite. The
next morning the doctor was
in his rostrum ready for us.

He told us, with some venom,
I thought, that he had made
arrangements for all of us to be
moved to various small hospitals
in the vicinity.

This announcement was received
with loud and continued applause
by some 500 laughing soldiers;
the doctor being so furious
that he left the rostrum where
he had

that small gate was opened, a crowd of laughing soldiers forced their way through, taking the doctor and porter with them, dashing straight towards where they were sleeping.

I suddenly remembered a back staircase (it could have been a fire escape) and used this for a quick entry to my ward, and hopped straight into bed, fully clothed and feigned sleep, just as the doctor and the sister came to inspect the "sleepers." All appeared sound asleep. It was dark and we got away with it, but not quite, the next morning the doctor who was in his rostrum was ready for us. He told us, with some venom, I thought, that he had made arrangements for all of us to be moved to various small hospitals in the vicinity.

This announcement was received with loud and continued applause by some 500 laughing soldiers; the doctor being so furious that he left the rostrum where he had

delivered his oration and left
the room in great indignation.

So we were all split up and
I was with a party who were
sent to a small cottage hospital
at Timperley; my new found
friends being sent to a hospital
at Whalley Range.

We all had a very enjoyable
at Timperley, the doctor in
charge being an ear, nose and
throat specialist who, on examination found that my nose had
completely grown together so that
I was breathing entirely through
my mouth.

So he kindly arranged for me
to see a surgeon in John Street
Manchester, who had to cut a
passage both sides of my nose so
that I could breathe properly.

After a further 3 weeks at this
nice hospital, visiting the Belle
Vue skating rink and Hippodrome,
being taken by car by a V.A.D.
nurse named Kilvert, who helped
at the hospital.

Then I left for home and ten
days hospital leave.

delivered his oration and left the room in great indignation.

So we were all split up and I was with a party who were sent to a small cottage hospital at Timperley; my new found friends being sent to a hospital at Whalley Range.

We all had a very enjoyable at Timperley, the doctor in charge being an ear, nose and throat specialist who, on examination found that my nose had completely grown together so that I was breathing entirely through my mouth.

So he kindly arranged for me to see a surgeon in John Street, Manchester, who had to cut a passage both sides of my nose so that I could breathe properly.

After a further 3 weeks at this nice hospital, visiting the Belle Vue Skating Rink and Hippodrome, being taken by car by a V.A.D. nurse named Kilvert, who helped at the hospital.

Then I left for home and ten days hospital leave.

Back to France Again

I spent two- to three months in England after being wounded in Delville Wood and, when returning to rejoin my unit, found they had been relieved by another regiment and were on the march to a village, well behind the front line, for a period of rest and training.

Forêt l'Abbaye was quite a large place and we all enjoyed the rest. We were there for Christmas, out of the line for the first time since arriving in France. It was arranged that "D" Company were to have their Christmas dinner in a large barn which had been cleared, trestles put up and suitably decorated.

Someone had told the Captain of our Company that I had a flair for lettering, so he sent for me and said he would be glad if I could paint two banners to be put up — one worded "WELCOME" and the other "GOD SAVE THE KING"...

12. Back to France again

I spent two to three months in England after being wounded in Delville Wood and, when returning to re-join my unit, found they had been relieved by another regiment and were on the march to a village well behind the front line for a period of rest and training.

Forêt L'Abbaye was quite a large place and we all enjoyed the rest. We were there for Christmas, out of the line for the first time since arriving in France. It was arranged that "D" Company were to have their Christmas dinner in a large barn which had been cleared, trestles put up and suitably decorated.

Someone had told the Captain of our company that I had a flair for lettering, so he sent for me and said he would be glad if I could paint two banners to be put up – one worded "WELCOME" and the other "GOD SAVE THE KING"...

The material with which I was
provided consisted of a roll of
wallpaper (lettering to go on the
plain side) and a large tube of
Sepia water-colour.

It turned out "being a very
convivial evening. A good deal
of French wine was drunk and
some whisky was smuggled
in for the occasion from "somewhere or other".

During dinner, the Captain
walked round wishing everyone "Happy Christmas". He was
then in a very jolly mood and
had a glass of wine in his
hand, sipping it as he came
along. When he reached me, he
said "Good old Bennett" (thinking
no doubt of the banners which
I had painted and now graced
the the ends of the barn); as he
said these words, without further
comment, he poured the wine
still in his glass over my head
and rubbed it in..

I heard later that, on his way
to his billet he walked straight
through the village pond...

A number of

The material with which I was provided consisted of a roll of wallpaper (lettering to go on the plain side) and a large tube of Sepia water-colour.

It turned out being a very convivial evening. A good deal of French wine was drunk and some whisky was smuggled in for the occasion from "somewhere or other."

During dinner, the Captain walked round wishing everyone "Happy Christmas." He was then in a very jolly mood and had a glass of wine in his hand, sipping it as he came long. When he reached me, he said "Good old Bennett" (thinking no doubt of the banners which I had painted and now graced the ends of the barn); as he said these words, without further comment, he poured the wine still in his glass over my head and rubbed it in...

I heard later that on his way to his billet he walked straight through the village pond...

A number of

the lads had a severe hangover next morning and a good
deal of "covering up" had to be
done.

There were no facilities for
a bath at this place, so next
morning, my friend borrowed
a wooden wash keeler from
the farm near by and we had
a cold, stand-up bath. It was
a sharp frost, but we rubbed
each other down vigourously
and felt fine after we had
dressed again. It makes one
shudder to think of it now.

When our rest period was over
we left Fôret l'Abbaye and
marched to Molliens du Bois
and then on to Nerf Moullen.
We spent several days at this
latter village and we able
to visit St. Omer, a large
town and quite a nice change.

Then we were on the move
again, this time to the Thiepval
area where we held the line
(10 days in and 10 out). On our
"out" periods, we were housed
in large "Nissen" huts; we were
bombed

the lads had a severe hangover next morning
and a good deal of "covering up" had to be
done.

There were no facilities for a bath at this place,
so next morning, my friend borrowed a wooden
wash keeler from the farm nearby and we had a
cold, stand up bath. It was a sharp frost, but we
rubbed each other down vigorously and felt fine
after we had dressed again. It makes one
shudder to think of it now.

When our rest period was over we left Forêt
L'Abbaye and marched to Molliens au Bois and
then on to Nerf Moullen. We spent several days
at this latter village and we [were] able to visit St
Omer, a large town and quite a nice change.

Then we were on the move again, this time to
the Thiepval area where we held the line (10
days in and 10 out). On our "out" periods, we
were housed in large "Nissen" huts; we were
bombed

on several occasions by single enemy aircraft in the early morning; we must have had some near misses, because we always had a shower of earth and a quantity of stones on the roof of our hut. They were after some long-range naval guns in the area; also an observation balloon unit.

We knew a young officer, called Basil Hallam in peaceful times, when he used to appear at the Hippodromes and Music Halls in all parts of the country. One of his songs was "I'm Gilbert the Filbert, the nut with the K." He was killed when his balloon caught fire when one of these raiding planes machine-gunned the balloon.

We missed him a lot, because during rest periods, he arranged some very good "shows" for our enjoyment.

The weather had now become very cold indeed; to give some idea, perhaps, fires had to be kept burning under the water cart on several occasions by single enemy aircraft in the early morning; we must have had some near misses, because we always had a shower of earth and a quantity of stones on the roof of our hut. They were after some long range naval guns in the area; also an observation balloon unit.

We knew a young officer, called Basil Hallam in peaceful times when he used to appear at the Hippodromes and Music Halls in all parts of the country. One of his songs was "I'm Gilbert the Filbert, the nut with the K". He was killed when his balloon caught fire when one of these raiding planes machine-gunned the balloon.

We missed him a lot, because during rest periods, he arranged some very good "shows" for our enjoyment.

The weather had now become very cold indeed, to give some idea perhaps fires had to be kept burning under the water cart

all the time, to keep the water
liquid. This cold continued for
six weeks with no fuel of
any kind to keep us warm. The
dead bodies of Germans killed
when the line we now held was
taken, were frozen into the earth
and were walked over every day.
   This is a fearful thing - but we
could do nothing at all about it.
On one occasion a few of us were
moved from our Nissen hut to
a ruined house and we thought
we might perhaps find some
odd wood lying about, so when
we saw some wooden shutters,
we thought that we would lift
these off their hinges and store
for firewood.
   Imagine our surprise when
we lifted them off. A lighted
candle was on a table and a
Frenchman inside ran out and
made enough noise to waken
the ded, calling for "La premiere
officaire de la Regiment". We
just disappeared into our ruined
house.
   One day, later on, whilst out
for a walk around, still looking
for wood

all the time, to keep the water liquid. This cold continued for six weeks with no fuel of any kind to keep us warm. The dead bodies of Germans killed when the line we now held was taken, were frozen in to the earth and were walked over every day.

This is a fearful thing, but we could do nothing at all about it. On one occasion a few of us were moved from our Nissen hut to a ruined house and we thought we might perhaps find some odd wood lying about, so when we saw some wooden shutters we thought that we would lift these off their hinges and store for firewood.

Imagine our surprise when we lifted them off. A lighted candle was on a table and a Frenchman inside ran out and made enough noise to waken the dead calling for "La premiere officaire de la regiment." We just disappeared into our ruined house.

One day, later on, whilst out for a walk around, still looking for wood

I saw that Brigade Headquarters had a large gate about 6 feet wide. On examination, it was one of the kind that could be lifted on and off. It was at this moment in time, that the idea was conceived of lifting it off and conveying to our billet to be used for firewood.

I also noticed that there were two military police on duty, and a sentry just outside the door. Watching the routine of the police, I found that when it became dark, one of them would walk about 100 yards down the road and light a cigarette.

Then the other policeman would walk down the road and join his partner; they both stayed there for 5 minutes, then the first one to go would return to his post just outside the gate, leaving the last one to continue his smoke. This we found was a routine procedure each night and there was thus, a period of five minutes when the gate was completely unguarded. The
sentry on the

I saw that Brigade Headquarters had a large gate about 6 feet wide. On examination, it was one of the kind that could be lifted on and off. It was at this moment in time that the idea was conceived of lifting it off and conveying to our billet to be used for firewood.

I also noticed that there were two military police on duty and a sentry just outside the door. Watching the routine of the police, I found that when it became dark, one of them would walk about 100 yards down the road and light a cigarette.

Then the other policeman would walk down the road and join his partner; they both stayed there for 5 minutes, then the first one to go would return to his post just outside the gate, leaving the last one to continue his smoke. This we found was a routine procedure each night and there was thus a period of five minutes when the gate was completely unguarded. The sentry on the

door we were not worried about
as the house was some distance
from the gate.

From all our deductions we
gathered that the gate would
have to be removed in well
under five minutes for the
operation to be successful. So
I suggested to the five lads
that it would make excellent
firewood and outlined my idea

Their first reaction was a laugh,
not thinking I was serious,
but when they found I _was_
serious they all thought I must
be mad, we might be court-
martialled for looting in war-
time. they were hesitant. but
I talked them into it.

So, when it was dark, away
we went, keeping well in the
shadows and watched the two
Military Police. Then, down the
road went policeman, No.1, Then
a flash appeared and that was
when he lit his cigarette. then
No.2 moved off. Then, we had to
move fast. Slipping silently up
to the gate, in two seconds we
had it off its hinges

door we were not worried about as the house was some distance from the gate.

From all our deductions we gathered that the gate would have to be removed in well under five minutes for the operation to be successful. So I suggested to the five lads that it would make excellent firewood and outlined my idea.

Their first reaction was a laugh, not thinking I was serious but when they found I <u>was</u> serious they all thought I must be mad, we might be court-martialled for looting in war time. They were hesitant, but I talked them into it.

So, when it was dark away we went, keeping well in the shadows and watched the two Military Police. Then, down the road went policeman No. 1, then a flash appeared and that was when he lit his cigarette. Then No. 2 moved off. Then, we had to move fast. Slipping silently up to the gate, in two seconds, we had it off its hinges

and keeping in the shadows of
the fence, all in step, moved
off in the direction of our billet
at a steady double! Not a word
had been spoken. Everything
went like clockwork. Then, all
at once, one of our number, a
rather highly-strung person,
appeared to see the funny side
to the adventure and let out
a peal of hysterical laughter.
I hissed at him "George,
you fool, you'll get us all in
the deep manure. Fortunately,
it was soon over, he just felt
he had to get rid of this feeling of laughter, and from
that moment, everything was
according to plan and we were
back in the billet.
We got our band saw out
and were soon working like
a team, getting the gate sawn
up into small pieces; we all
thought there might be some
repercussions when those M.P.'s
missed the gate, but we
never heard a whisper about
it; the wood was hidden in a
cellar underneath

and keeping in the shadows of the fence, all in step, moved off in the direction of our billet at a steady double. Not a word had been spoken. Everything went like clockwork. Then, all at once, one of our number, a rather highly-strung person appeared to see the funny side to the adventure and let out a peal of hysterical laughter. I hissed at him "George you fool, you'll get us all in the deep manure." Fortunately, it was soon over, he just felt he had to get rid of this feeling of laughter, and from that moment, everything was according to plan and we were back in the billet.

We got our band saw out and were soon working like a team, getting the gate sawn up into small pieces; we all thought there might be some repercussions when those M.P.'s missed the gate, but we never heard a whisper about it; the wood was hidden in a cellar underneath the house. However, there was a billet inspection a few days after, but it was probably just a routine occasion.

But, in a roundabout way, we had to pay for the gate: The French Government sent in a claim to our Division for 3000 fruit trees, which had been cut down for firewood, during this very cold spell in February, 1917, so the military authorities decided to stop a small amount out of every man's pay in the Division to cover the loss.

There had recently been some very heavy fighting in the area and men who had been killed were still lying there, frozen stiff under the snow, waiting for a thaw, so that they could be buried.

In the line dead Germans were frozen into the ground and we had to walk over them when going to and fro. The cold was so intense that, one morning, after I had drawn our platoon's rum the house. However, there was a billet inspection a few days after, but it was probably just a routine occasion.

But, in a roundabout way, we had to pay for the gate: the French Government sent in a claim to our Division for 3000 fruit trees, which had been cut down for firewood, during this very cold spell in February 1917, so the military authorities decided to stop a small amount out of every man's pay in the Division to cover the loss.

* * * * *

There had recently been some very heavy fighting in the area and men who had been killed were still lying there, frozen stiff under the snow, waiting for a thaw, so that they could be buried.

In the line dead Germans were frozen into the ground and we had to walk over them when going to and fro. The cold was so intense that, one morning, after I had drawn our platoon's rum

rum ration in a tin, I had to literally peel my fingers off the tin – a little more and they would have been frozen.

After our ten-day period in the line, we would walk out in twos and threes, so that the enemy should not be able to say, for certain, just when the troops were being relieved.

The roads were so slippery that one generally slipped and fell at least once on this journey out of the line. Sometimes, a man would really suffer an injury.

I fell one night and, in falling, my rifle caught me a severe blow on my head and really shook me up. As I lay in the road for a moment, before getting up, suddenly a head appeared out of a hole near the road and a voice said: "Would you like some hot pea soup?"

I never enjoyed anything so much in my life. This heaven-sent gift was dispensed to us by members of the Society of Friends, who were non-combatants, but, nevertheless, ration in a tin, I had to literally peel my fingers off the tin – a little more and they would have been frozen.

After our ten-day period in the line, we would walk out in twos and threes so that the enemy should not be able to say, for certain, just when the troops were being relieved.

The roads were so slippery that one generally slipped and fell at least once on this journey out of the line. Sometimes a man would really suffer an injury.

I fell one night and in falling my rifle caught me a severe blow on my head and really shook me up. As I lay in the road for a moment, before getting up, suddenly a head appeared out of a hole near the road and a voice said: "Would you like some hot pea soup?"

I never enjoyed anything so much in my life. This heaven-sent gift was dispensed to us by members of the Society of Friends, who were non-combatants, but, nevertheless, were in an area, where death could strike at any moment.

From that moment we had a very different idea, of those kindly folks, who were doing everything in their power to lessen the hardships of those whose duty it was to kill the enemy whenever possible.

We never really gave it much thought, but I cannot recall ever hating the Germans. We knew they were committed to this "killing" in the protection of the Fatherland. Privately, I often felt that the war could have been avoided, if everyone had tried a little harder.

We often thought of vanished comforts, enjoyed in the pre-war years - of slippers, an armchair, and a smoke by the fire.

As I once heard a young officer, who was in the line for the first time, on a wet, misty day and, as I passed his dugout, he exclaimed in a loud voice: "Woe is me, wretched man that I am". He was speaking for all of us, just then...

were in an area where death could strike at any moment.

From that moment we had a very different idea of those kindly folks, who were doing everything in their power to lessen the hardships of those whose duty it was to kill the enemy whenever possible.

We never really gave it much thought, but I cannot recall ever hating the Germans. We knew they were committed to this "killing" in the protection of the Fatherland. Privately, I often felt that the war could have been avoided, if everyone had tried a little harder.

We often thought of vanished comforts, enjoyed in the pre-war years – of slippers, an armchair, and a smoke by the fire.

As I once heard a young officer who was in the line for the first time, on a wet misty day and, as I passed his dugout he exclaimed in a loud voice: "Woe is me, wretched man that I am!" He was speaking for all of us, just then…

The Attack on the Ancre Front

Shortly after several weeks of line duties we marched back to a village named Hédaville. where we were put through some field training in readiness for an attack in the River Ancre area.

Whilst we were on our way to the front line, a rapid thaw set in and the whole place was a sea of mud, with all the dead bodies, frozen stiff for some six weeks, lying just as they had fallen. As we passed by we were astonished to see so many men lying in such close proximity to each other and wondered what could have happened.

Maybe a mine caught them as they were on line of march - We shall never know!

We were in active support to the Suffolk Regiment, who were making the attack. We took up our positions on the slope of a hill. Information reached us

13. The attack on the Ancre front

Shortly after several weeks of line duties we marched back to a village named Hédaville, where we were put through some field training in readiness for an attack in the River Ancre area.

Whilst we were on our way to the front line, a rapid thaw set in and the whole place was a sea of mud; with all the dead bodies, frozen stiff for some six weeks, lying just as they had fallen. As we passed by we were astonished to see so many men lying in such close proximity to each other and wondered what could have happened.

Maybe a mine caught them as they were on line of march – we shall never know!

We were in active support to the Suffolk Regiment, who were making the attack. We took up our positions on the slope of a hill. Information reached us

that the "Suffolks" has reached
their objective and were now
consolidating their position.
  We thus had to act as a supply
unit and kept them supplied
with all their requirements,
munitions, food, water, losing
a number of men, killed and
wounded during the period we
were there, mostly from shell fire.
I was acting as a corporal at this
time, owing to a short of N.C.O.s,
and the Company Officer sent for
me and explained that the
"Suffolks", who were in the front
line, were short of water and he
wanted me to take charge of a
water-carrying party.
  It was now about 11 p.m. and
was instructed to go by way of
"Boom" ravine, which would give
a measure of protection against both
small arms and artillery fire. I
had heard of this place and
wondered why it had this very
curious name. That was something
we found out later on.
  The names of the men forming
the carrying party were given to
                            me and

that the "Suffolks" had reached their objective and were now consolidating their position.

We thus had to act as a supply unit and kept them supplied with all their requirements, munitions, food, water, losing a number of men, killed and wounded during the period we were there, mostly from shell fire.

I was acting as a corporal at this time, owing to a short[age] of N.C.O.s and the Company Officer sent for me and explained that the "Suffolks," who were in the front line, we[re] short of water and he wanted me to take charge of a water-carrying party.

It was now about 11 p.m. and [I] was instructed to go by way of "Boom" ravine, which would give a measure of protection against both small arms and artillery fire. I had heard of this place and wondered why it had this very curious name. That was something we found out later on.

The names of the men forming the carrying party were given to me and

I proceeded to collect them from their various dug-outs. There were bursts of heavy artillery fire at intervals all the time and I was anxious to get going. Four of the men came out as soon as their name was called, but two of them would not come out owing to the heavy enemy artillery fire; meanwhile, we were out in the open, throwing ourselves down frequently. Finally, I had to send for the sergeant-major, and he had to threaten them with a court-martial, "unless they came out at once."

Eventually, they did and the rest of us took a dim view of their behaviour.

Personally, I didn't much care to have charge of soldiers who had shown themselves to have such a low morale.

Dugouts, however, tend to give personnel a feeling of insecurity when they have to leave their shelter.

I proceeded to collect them from their various dugouts. There were bursts of heavy artillery fire at intervals all the time and I was anxious to get going. Four of the men came out as soon as their name was called, but two of them would not come out owing to the heavy enemy artillery fire, meanwhile, we were out in the open, throwing ourselves down frequently. Finally, I had to send for the sergeant major and he had to threaten them with a court-martial "unless they came out at once."

Eventually, they did and the rest of us took a dim view of their behaviour.

Personally, I didn't much care to have charge of soldiers who had shown themselves to have such a low morale.

Dugouts, however, tend to give personnel a feeling of insecurity when they have to leave their shelter.

"Boom" Ravine

With all the waiting about, it must have been midnight before we really "were on our way". We had a "guide" as far as the entrance to the "Ravine".

It was about eight yards wide at the bottom with "cliffs" sloping slightly upwards to some 20-25 feet. We had not proceeded far before "Jerry" started to drop shells neatly into the ravine and, when they were near, we had to drop down.

As we put our hands on the ground, we found that some barbed wire had be pegged down, so that our hands and ankles were being torn on this devilish device. No-one had told us about this hazard in advance.

All this slowed down our progress as we had to pay more attention where we put our feet and take more care of our hands when dropping down. It was a dreadful journey and one which is never forgotten...

14. "Boom" Ravine

With all the waiting about it must have been midnight before we really "were on our way." We had a "guide" as far as the entrance to the "Ravine."

It was about eight yards wide at the bottom with "cliffs" sloping slightly upwards to some 20-25 feet. We had not proceeded far before "Jerry" started to drop shells neatly into the ravine and, when they were near we had to drop down.

As we put our hands on the ground, we found that some barbed wire had be[en] pegged down so that our hands and ankles were being torn on this devilish device. No-one had told us about this hazard in advance.

All this slowed down our progress as we had to pay more attention where we put our feet and take more care of our hands when dropping down. It was a dreadful journey and one which is never forgotten...

We were almost at end of the journey, when a shell dropped very close, and we had to throw ourselves down quickly.

When we got up again, I called out the names of the party, to see if everyone was OK, but one never answered. We all called out his name and searched, as best we could (as it was pitch dark) but we found no trace of him at all, and concluded he must have received a direct hit.

So we went on and hoped that he had been wounded, and was making his way back to base.

We arrived at the "Suffolk" headquarters and received a "chit" from the officer-in-charge for the cans of water (less two that the missing man was carrying. Now we had to get back to our unit, but, I said, by way of "Boom" Ravine."

It was now about two o'clock in the morning and we started on our way back over the top

                                    We extended

"Boom" Ravine

We were almost at [the] end of the journey when a shell dropped very close and we had to throw ourselves down quickly.

When we got up again, I called out the names of the party to see if everyone was OK, but one never answered. We all called out his name and searched as best we could (as it was pitch dark) but we found no trace of him at all and concluded he must have received a direct hit.

So we went on and hoped that he had been wounded and was making his way back to base.

We arrived at the "Suffolk" headquarters and received a "chit" from the officer-in-charge for the cans of water (less two that the missing man was carrying). Now we had to get back to our unit, but [not*], I said, by way of "Boom" Ravine.

* * * * *

It was now about two o'clock in the morning and we started on our way back over the top. We extended

The following section only makes sense if they do not *go back through "Boom" Ravine.*

ourselves, so that if a shell came
near, it was unlikely that all
would suffer an injury, but,
the going was very difficult.
There were no duckboards and
the ground was just a sea of
mud, with frequent shell holes
which one never saw until it
was too late for evasive action.

We had some idea of direction,
by listening to the sounds of
the machine-guns, which were
quite different and this, at any
rate, gave us a good idea of
which was "ours or theirs".

We must have walked miles
more than we need have done,
trying to avoid shell holes
and small pits of water. It
was early morning (about 6 a.m)
when the five of the carrying
parties and myself arrived back
with the company. Everyone
was completely wet through and
thoroughly exhausted.

We had no hot drinks to cheer
us up on our arrival; reporting
the loss of one man and two cans
of water and handing the "chit"
for the receipt of the water just
a murmured "good show".   ...

ourselves, so that if a shell came near, it was unlikely that all would suffer an injury, but the going was very difficult. There were no duckboards and the ground was just a sea of mud, with frequent shell holes which one never saw until it was too late for evasive action.

We had some idea of direction, by listening to the sounds of the machine guns, which were quite different and this, at any rate gave us a good idea of which was "ours or theirs."

We must have walked miles more than we need have done trying to avoid shell holes and small pits of water. It was early morning (about 6 a.m.) when the five of the carrying party and myself arrived back with the company. Everyone was completely wet through and thoroughly exhausted.

We had no hot drinks to cheer us up on our arrival; reporting the loss of one man and two cans of water and handing the "chit" for the receipt of the water, just a murmured "Good Show!"...

Sent to Hospital with Trench Fever

After a few more days in the support area, we were moved to some dugouts in the Reserve Area. It was late afternoon when we arrived and, once inside the dugout, we just laid down and fell fast asleep with all our equipment on. This was the first real sleep we had enjoyed for over 3 days, and we all slept soundly.

On awaking next morning, we slipped off our equipment and were waiting for "tea" and the breakfast meal. I tried to stand up, but fell down and my head was throbbing madly, and everything seemed blurred, so I reported "sick" and, with a number of others, were lined up and started off on our way to the doctor's tent...

Just then, an enemy shell dropped quite close and sent the "sick" parade off at a steady double. Now I was quite alone, and could just "drag" myself along. It was quite half-an-hour before

120

15. Sent to hospital with trench fever

After a few more days in the support area, we were moved to some dugouts in the Reserve Area. It was late afternoon when we arrived and once inside the dugout, we just laid down and fell fast asleep with all our equipment on. This was the first real sleep we had enjoyed for over 3 days and we all slept soundly.

On awaking next morning, we slipped off our equipment and were waiting for "tea" and the breakfast meal. I tried to stand up, but fell down and my head was throbbing madly and everything seemed blurred, so I reported "sick" and, with a number of others, were lined up and started off on our way to the doctors tent…

Just then, an enemy shell dropped quite close and sent the "sick" parade off at a steady double. Now I was quite alone, and could just "drag" myself along. It was quite half-an-hour before

I reached the M.O.'s tent. He gave
me a thorough examination and told
me I had trench fever and had
a temperature of 103°. Arrangements
were made for me to be taken by
ambulance to the nearest field
hospital, where I was undressed
and put straight to bed. The next
morning my temperature was still
103°, so I was sent to a base hospital at Le Tréport (the old
Trianon Hotel in peace-time),
and put straight to bed, after
having my temperature taken
again.

Next morning, a military
doctor came round early to have
a look at the trench fever cases.
Without more than a cursory
glance at each one, he just tapped
their beds as he passed each one,
calling out "Up", "Up", "Up", and so
on right through the ward. The
sister was trying to tell him we
all had high temperatures but
he took no notice and ordered
that we be put on scrubbing
tables, or similar work.

It was quite an effort for me
to stand up

I reached the M.O.'s tent. He gave me a thorough examination and told me I had trench fever and had a temperature of 103°. Arrangements were made for me to be taken by ambulance to the nearest field hospital, where I was undressed and put straight to bed. The next morning my temperature was still 103°, so I was sent to a base hospital at Le Treport (the old Trianon Hotel in peace-time), and put straight to bed, after having my temperature taken again.

Next morning a military doctor came round early to have a look at the trench fever cases. Without more than a cursory glance at each one, he just tapped their beds as he passed each one calling out "Up, up, up," and so on right through the ward. The sister was trying to tell him we all had high temperatures but he took no notice and ordered that we be put on scrubbing tables, or similar work.

It was quite an effort for me to stand up

apart from scrubbing tables and after a few minutes on my feet, went off in a "dead" faint and when I came round, found a nurse patting my cheeks. Then she took my temperature again and it was still 103°.

And, that is how it was for the fourteen days I was there: up in the mornings and down at night. One night it went down to seven degrees below normal, and, for several days could not be moved.

Then, a visiting doctor decided I must be sent to England for special treatment. But, there was some delay, because, it was found that all the patients in the hospital were infected with lice. This was traced to the French people who had been doing the laundry for the hospital, and an orderly had to go round removing all their hair from their bodies.

x x x x x x

apart from scrubbing tables and after a few minutes on my feet, went off in a "dead" faint and when I came round, found a nurse patting my cheeks. Then she took my temperature again and it was still 103°.

And, that is how it was for the fourteen days I was there: up in the mornings and down at night. One night it went down to seven degrees below normal, and, for several days could not be moved.

Then, a visiting doctor decided I must be sent to England for special treatment. But, there was some delay because it was found that all the patients in the hospital were infected with lice. This was traced to the French people who had been doing the laundry for the hospital, and an orderly had to go round removing all hair from their bodies.

By Boat to England and arrival in Scotland

I was still a stretcher case and the sick and wounded were taken by ambulance to the hospital ship which was taking us over to "blighty". I have no recollection of the port where we embarked, or the name of the ship, but can just remember long periods of sickness on the journey over. I was in bed all the time and felt awful.

An orderly came and asked me the name of my home town, I told him "Norwich, Norfolk, but after a long train journey, we were taken to an hospital at Paisley, in Scotland, where I had to be taken by stretcher up a winding staircase to the ward which was to be my home for nearly 90 days. A very uncomfortable and frightening experience.

Several days passed before I was able to take any notice of anything . . .

16. By boat to England and arrival in Scotland

I was still a stretcher case and the sick and wounded were taken by ambulance to the hospital ship which was taking us over to "blighty." I have no recollection of the port where we embarked or the name of the ship, but can just remember long periods of sickness on the journey over. I was in bed all the time and felt awful.

An orderly came and asked me the name of my home town, I told him "Norwich, Norfolk", but after a long train journey, we were taken to a hospital at Paisley in Scotland, where I had to be taken by stretcher up a winding staircase to the ward which was to be my home for nearly 90 days. A very uncomfortable and frightening experience.

Several days passed before I was able to take any notice of anything...

but what a different atmosphere.
Trained nurses, helped by V.A.Ds.
did everything possible for the
recovery of the patients, and
we even had visitors who came
regularly to see us on the visiting
days. The first one, however,
was a miserable day for me,
as I was the only English soldier
on the ward, but, it was the
start of my numerous visitors. A
Scotch lady, who was visiting her
son in the next bed to me, came
over to me and said "Puir wee
laddie, an' ye got no-one
ter visit ye!" "I'll bring a
bonny wee lassie to see ye
next visiting day."
    I was worried, somewhat by
this reference to "a bonny wee
lassie", as I was married then
and could see some dreadful
situations arising; but I
need not have worried, she
was already "engaged" and
both she and her fiancé
came regularly all the while
I was there...
    Strangely enough, down in
Norwich, my wife's people had
some...

but what a different atmosphere. Trained nurses, helped by V.A.D.s did everything possible for the recovery of the patients and we even had visitors who came regularly to see us on the visiting days. The first one, however was a miserable day for me as I was the only English soldier on the ward, but it was the start of my numerous visitors. A Scotch lady, who was visiting her son in the next bed to me, came over to me and said "Puir wee laddie an ye got no-one ter visit ye!. I'll bring a bonny wee lassie to see ye next visiting day."

I was worried somewhat by this reference to a "bonny wee lassie," as I was married then and could see some dreadful situation arising but I need not have worried, she was already "engaged" and both she and her fiancé came regularly all the while I was there...

Strangely enough, down in Norwich, my wife's people had some...

Scottish soldiers billeted with
them, and hearing I was in
hospital at Paisley, wrote to
their parents and said I would
appreciate a visit from them.
Altogether, there was never
a visiting day for me, without
a visitor to make it complete;
and, they always brought me
some little thing — cigarettes, cakes
or eggs.

The hospital doctor was an
ideal family doctor, named
Adam and the nurses were
kind and considerate. One of
the patients was a Sergeant.
Cheetham. He had wounds in
both his feet and, when he was
well enough, they would put
him in a wheel-chair and
take him for a bath. One
morning, however, there was
a disaster, the nurse who was
pushing his chair, slipped on
the highly-polished floor and
fell, releasing her hold on his
chair, which went forward at
ever-increasing speed. The
unfortunate sergeant yelled as
he found ...

Scottish soldiers billeted with them and hearing I was in hospital at Paisley, wrote to their parents and said I would appreciate a visit from them.

Altogether there was never a visiting day for me without a visitor to make it complete; and, they always brought me some little thing – cigarettes, cakes or eggs.

The hospital doctor was an ideal family doctor, named Adam and the nurses were kind and considerate. One of the patients was a Sergeant Cheatham. He had wounds in both his feet and, when he was well enough, they would put him in a wheel-chair and take him for a bath. One morning, however, there was a disaster, the nurse who was pushing his chair slipped on a highly polished floor and fell, releasing her hold on his chair, which went forward at ever increasing speed. The unfortunate sergeant yelled as he found...

himself heading straight for
the hot-water pipes at the end
of the ward, where he finally
came to rest with his bandaged
feet pressed against the pipes.
The sergeant yelled and swore
until the nurses ran to remove
the chair and his feet from
the pipes. Truly a case where
the term: "My feet are killing
me" can be aptly employed.

It was, altogether a very nice
hospital and staff, were excellent;
a pleasant period, but a long
one for me, as the fever had
affected my heart and, every time
the nurses tried to get me up for
a change, I collapsed. Finally,
the doctor put me in a small
ward, just for one person and
I spent a fortnight there, until
I was able to get up and sit in
a chair.

From that time everything went
well and it was possible to go out
and see something of Paisley.
It had been a very cold winter,
with a heavy snowfall on the
Easter Monday (April 5): it was
now April 27th...

himself heading straight for the hot-water pipes at the end of the ward, where he finally came to rest with his bandaged feet pressed against the pipes.

The sergeant yelled and swore until the nurses ran to remove the chair and his feet from the pipes. Truly a case where the term: "My feet are killing me" can be aptly employed.

It was altogether a very nice hospital and staff were excellent; a pleasant period but a long one for me, as the fever had affected my heart and every time the nurses tried to get me up for a change, I collapsed. Finally, the doctor put me in a small ward, just for one person and I spent a fortnight there until I was able to get up and sit in a chair.

From that time everything went well and it was possible to go out and see something of Paisley. It had been a very cold winter, with a heavy snowfall on the Easter Monday (April 5); it was now April 27th ...

and much warmer, so several folks
asked me round to tea, generally
accompanied by one of the staff,
as they were still a bit nervous
about my health. On one occasion
I went to the Hippodrome with a
party of convalescing wounded men,
with tea later at a café.

Then, the doctor came round
one morning and said I would
be fit to go home on leave the
next week, so I reported to the
army quartermaster and asked
if I could have my clothing and
belongings, but one can imagine
my surprise when he told me I
had no trousers.

All my belongings had followed
me all the way from the field
hospital at Bray-sur-Somme to
Pairley hospital in Scotland;
somewhere, someone must have
"swiped" my "bags", together with
a gold watch (wristlet) and several
treasured possessions, including a
gold signet engagement ring —
a present from my wife
and a gold locket with my
wife's photograph inside...

and much warmer, so several folks asked me round to tea, generally accompanied by one of the staff, as they were still a bit nervous about my health. On one occasion I went to the Hippodrome with a party of convalescing wounded men, with tea later at a café.

Then, the doctor came round one morning and said I would be fit to go home on leave the next week, so I reported to the army quartermaster and asked if I could have my clothing and belongings but one can imagine my surprise when he told me I had no trousers.

All my belongings had followed me all the way from the field hospital at Bray-sur-Somme to Paisley hospital in Scotland; somewhere someone must have "swiped" my "bags," together with a gold watch (wristlet) and several treasured possessions, including a gold signet engagement ring – a present from my wife and a gold locket with my wife's photograph inside…

I felt very upset about my trousers and contents, but he said, "don't worry about the trousers the army would supply me with another pair and deduct the cost from my account." I protested that I had not lost the trousers as I had been in bed in hospital since I left the field hospital at Foray - sur - Somme, so could not be responsible for their loss.

I was feeling rather mad about losing my personal belongings, as well as being "de-bagged" and argued a good deal that the authorities were responsible and not <u>me</u> and that they should be responsible and bear the cost of a new pair of trousers, but, the "quarter-bloke" who sympathised with me, said that it was an army rule and nothing could be done about it and I would have to pay.

I accepted this in the end and eventually left the hospital for 10 days leave.

It was a nerve-wracking train ride until we reached Perth, where...

I felt very upset about my trousers and contents, but he said, "don't worry about the trousers the army would supply me with another pair and deduct the cost from my account." I protested that I had not lost the trousers as I had been in bed in hospital since I left the field hospital at Bray-sur-Somme, so could not be responsible for their loss.

I was feeling rather mad about losing my personal belongings, as well as being "de-bagged," and argued a good deal that the authorities were responsible and not <u>me</u> and that they should be responsible and bear the cost of a new pair of trousers but the "quarter-bloke" who sympathised with me, said that it was an Army rule and nothing could be done about it and I would have to pay.

I accepted this in the end and eventually left the hospital for 10 days leave.

It was a nerve-wracking train ride until we reached Perth, where...

me had to change. There were
a number of delays on the
way down to Euston station,
where we arrived too late to
catch the last train from
Siverpool Street station for home
run to "Norwich Thorpe".

Consequently, we were shown
a Church of England hostel just
outside the station where for
a small charge, one could stay
the night (this was Saturday).
It appeared that the hostel must
have had "resident" fleas, as on
awakening during the night,
found myself covered with
flea-bites. After being so long
in bed, my body must have
been quite a delicacy for these
insects.

Next morning, we found that
the first train for Norwich
left at 9 a.m. and were told
we should have to walk the
journey, as no buses were
running on Sundays. The
streets were absolutely deserted,
just the odd milk cart now
and then, so we got on the home
train and were on our way...

138

we had to change. There were a number of delays on the way down to Euston station, where we arrived too late to catch the last train from Liverpool Street Station for home run to "Norwich, Thorpe."

Consequently, we were shown a Church of England hostel just outside the station where for a small charge, one could stay the night (this was Saturday). It appeared that the hostel must have had "resident" fleas, as on awakening during the night found myself covered with flea bites. After being so long in bed, my body must have been quite a delicacy for these insects.

Next morning, we found that the first train for Norwich left at 9 a.m. and were told we should have to walk the journey, as no buses were running on Sundays. The streets were absolutely deserted, just the odd milk cart now and then, so we got on the home train and were on our way…

"Once more into the Breach"...

The ten days leave passed all too quickly, and, after the usual "hurricane" visits to our friends and relations, seeing a few shows etc, & reported to the Britannia barracks, where, I was given a job as Sergeants Mess Orderly. I did this for a fortnight and, finally, a party of us were sent to Shoreham convalescent camp, where they tried to "harden" us off again, in readiness for the next round

We spent a month here and were sent at the end to a large tent for "medical" inspection.

This was an absolute "farce". We passed in single file past an army doctor, who was sitting at a table about 5 yards away, and, as our names and numbers were called out, he looked at our medical sheets and called out "A1", and the orderly marked this in a record book. This was the usual procedure, the old soldiers "on the staff told me afterwards

17. "Once more into the breach..."

The ten days leave passed all too quickly and after the usual "hurricane" visits to our friends and relations, seeing a few shows etc., I reported to the Britannia barracks where I was given a job as Sergeants Mess orderly. I did this for a fortnight and finally a party of us were sent to Shoreham Convalescent Camp where they tried to "harden" us off again in readiness for the next round.

We spent a month here and were sent at the end to a large tent for "medical" inspection.

This was an absolute "farce." We passed in single file past an army doctor who was sitting at a table about 5 yards away and as our names and numbers were called out, he looked at our medical sheets and called out "A1," and the orderly marked this in a record book. This was the usual procedure the old soldiers on the staff told me afterwards...

So we were all fit men again, after an examination from about five yards distant. We were all thoroughly disgusted, and had to accept this decision with resignation.

The P.B.I. are a long-suffering race and, finally, I reported to the 3rd (Feeding) Battalion Norfolk Regiment at Felixstowe (Suffolk) where after a period of hard, intensive training, was soon travelling down to Southampton to embark for France, joining the Battalion in Belgium (Arnecke) in late August, 1917.

x   x   x   x

The 8th Norfolk Regt, at this time, were "resting" at a village called Arnecke, near Cassell, an Army Headquarters in Belgium. The weather was rather warm by day, but cold at night; the Regiment was under canvas at first, but later, had billets in various farm premises in the area. The nights were not very peaceful, however, and, air raids were frequent during the hours of darkness.

"Once more into the breach..."

So we were all fit men again after an examination from about 5 yards distant. We were all thoroughly disgusted and had to accept this decision with resignation.

The P.B.I. are a long suffering race and finally, I reported to the 3rd (Feeding) Battalion Norfolk Regiment at Felixstowe (Suffolk), where, after a period of hard intensive training, was soon travelling down to Southampton to embark for France joining the Battalion in Belgium (Arnecke) in late August, 1917.

* * * * *

The 8th Norfolk Regt, at this time, were "resting" at a village called Arnecke, near Cassell, an army headquarters in Belgium. The weather was rather warm by day but cold at night; the Regiment was under canvas at first, but later had billets in various farm premises in the area. The nights were not very peaceful, however, and air raids were frequent during the hours of darkness.

Many times we had some "near misses", when clods of earth descended on the roof of our "Nissen" hut, where we moved for a week before occupying the big barn, which was quite near to the farmer's house. and his wife often cooked meals for a "selected" few, and, in return, we would often hand her a tin of jam or "bully" beef.

When I was visiting them one day, it was quite a sight to see the children, in their "jeans", sitting round the table, and "giving thanks" for a plate of cold, "bully" beef.

It was now about harvest-time, and beans as well as corn would soon be "gathered in". The farmer's son, a big, tall, Poilu had been given a long leave from the Army, so that he could go home and help with the harvest.

One day, when he was on top of a corn stack, one of our fellows, who had been

drinking more

144

"Once more into the breach..."

Many times we had some "near misses," when clods of earth descended on the roof of our "Nissen" hut, where we moved for a week before occupying the big barn, which was quite near to the farmer's house, and his wife often cooked meals for a "selected" few and in return we would often hand her a tin of jam or "bully" beef.

When I was visiting them one day, it was quite a sight to see the children in their "jeans" sitting round the table and "giving thanks" for a plate of cold "bully" beef.

* * * * *

It was now about harvest time and beans as well as corn would soon be "gathered in." The farmer's son, a big tall Poilu* had been given a long leave from the army, so that he could go home and help with the harvest.

One day, when he was on top of a corn stack, one of our fellows, who had been drinking more...

*Poilu: literally 'hairy,' indicating unshaven, unkempt; common French term for an ordinary soldier at the time.

French wine than was good for him, shouted some remark to the "Poilu" as he lurched past, but I was not near enough to hear what it was, but it must have been insulting, as the Frenchman didn't like it at all, with the persistence of a drunken man, he repeated his remark and this time I was near enough to hear him say: "You're a b—— Boche."

Nothing could have been more inflammatory to a French soldier, just home on leave from the front line, than a remark like that.

That did it! The Poilu was soon down from the stack, and, getting his pitchfork at the ready, charged straight at our drunken friend, who, sensing his danger, legged it over the large meadow as if he were jet-propelled.

Fellows came out of the billet and cheered at the incident, but "Tommy" kept on running, not once looking back; he was now quite sober...

"Once more into the breach..."

French wine than was good for him, shouted
some remark to the "Poilu" as he lurched past,
but I was not near enough to hear what it was
but it must have been insulting, as the
Frenchman didn't like it at all. With the
persistence of a drunken man, he repeated this
remark and this time I was near enough to hear
him say: "You're a b----- Boche."

Nothing could have been more inflammatory
to a French soldier just home on leave from the
front line than a remark like that.

That did it! The Poilu was soon down from
the stack, and getting his pitchfork at the ready,
charged straight at our drunken friend, who,
sensing his danger, legged it over the large
meadow as if he were jet-propelled.

Fellows came out of the billet and cheered at
the incident, but Tommy kept on running, not
once looking back; he was now quite sober…

but the Poilu soon returned
to his job on the stack. Honour
had been satisfied! and the
incident became forgotten, as
good relations became quickly
resumed.

We were on the move again
shortly after the foregoing
incident, and, after a rather
long march, arrived at a village
much nearer the front line,
called St Jan ter Biezen, where
we did a lot of manœuvres.

Here refugees from the "front
line" villages, had built homes
for themselves from odd wood
and army biscuit tins. The most
curious looking street I have
ever seen anywhere.

There were many good houses
and shops, also an estaminet,
called "Soliel d'Or". There was
a beerhouse, more like an
English pub" than anything
I had ever seen out there. This
building had sandbags as
high as the eaves all round,
whilst the customers drank
their beer outside, sheltered by
the sand-bagged house.

but the Poilu soon returned to his job on the stack. Honour had been satisfied! and the incident became forgotten as good relations became quickly resumed.

We were on the move again shortly after the foregoing incident and after a rather long march arrived at a village much nearer the front line, called St Jan ter Biezen, where we did a lot of manoeuvres.

Here refugees from the "front line" villages had built homes for themselves from odd wood and army biscuit tins. The most curious looking street I have ever seen anywhere.

There were many good houses and shops, also an estaminet called "Soleil d'Or." There was a beer house more like an English "pub" than anything I had ever seen out there. This building had sandbags as high as the eaves all round, whilst the customers drank their beer outside sheltered by the sand-bagged house.

It was here, whilst doing field training, that my friend and I were asked if we would consider taking on the responsibility of becoming an officer. We said we would like a little time to think about it.

After a talk about the proposal, we finally said; we would be willing to go to an officer's training unit to receive training for this position. It was not an easy decision to make as it was a recognised thing for a junior officers life to be limited to fourteen days.

Our names were taken and we were told that we should hear about it later.

We knew at this time, that our field training was to fit us for a large operation in the "Passchendaele" area, which was to be launched before the wet weather set in. At the time of our training, the hot dry time was ideal for any advance likely to be made in the area which has just been mentioned.

"Once more into the breach..."

It was here, whilst doing field training that my friend and I were asked if we would consider taking on the responsibility of becoming an officer. We said we would like a little time to think about it.

After a talk about the proposal, we finally said: we would be willing to go to an officers' training unit to receive training for this position. It was not an easy decision to make as it was a recognised thing for a junior officer's life to be limited to fourteen days.

Our names were taken and we were told that we should hear about it later.

We knew at this time, that our field training was to fit us for a large operation in the "Passendaele" area which was to be launched before the wet weather set in. At the time of our training the hot dry time was ideal for any advance likely to be made in the area which has just been mentioned.

Every day in the St. Jan ter Biezen
area, "Jerry" would fire, at a regular
hour, a single shell of very large
calibre (said to be 18 inch) and we
generally had warning of this, as,
when the wind was right, it
was possible to hear a "clang"
as the gun was fired.

Poperinghe was one of the
principal targets, as a host of
transport, men and materials
passed through this place daily.
It was also an important railhead.
One day, as a party of men from
the 18th Division were waiting
for the train to arrive which
would convey them to Le Havre.
to catch a leave boat to "Blighty",
(there were 42 men in the party)
one of these 18 inch shells
dropped only a short distance
away, killing 14 men and
wounding many others. This was
a great tragedy, as many of the
men had been out in France
for two years, without seeing
their families.

x   x   x   x

"Once more into the breach..."

Every day in the St. Jan ter Biezen area "Jerry" would fire at a regular hour, a single shell of very large calibre (said to be 18 inch) and we generally had warning of this, as when the wind was right it was possible to hear a "clang" as the gun was fired.

Poperinghe was one of the principal targets, as a host of transport, men and materials passed through this place daily. It was also an important railhead. One day, as a party of men from the 18th division were waiting for the train to arrive which would convey them to Le Havre to catch a leave boat to "Blighty" (there were 42 men in the party) one of these 18 inch shells dropped only a short distance away, killing 14 men and wounding many others. This was a great tragedy as many of the men had been out in France for two years, without seeing their families.

The Passchendaele affair!

It was a lovely sunny day in October as we moved out of St Jan ter Baizen on the first "leg" of our journey to "the line".

We passed through Vlamertinghe, and St. Julien and, all the time, the countryside became more war-ravaged and menacing. ~~It was a great revelation to me to see large numbers of tanks lying helpless on one side in a rather marshy area, just before reaching the Menin Road~~. The battalion stayed near the bridge in some deep dug outs on one side and a large field hospital on the other, fully staffed with doctors and nurses.

Next morning as we were getting ready to continue our journey to the line, I was stung twice by wasps in about ten minutes of each other; the place was "alive" with wasps, all of them in a semi-"intoxicated" condition.

There were a number of enemy reconnaissance planes

18. The Passchendaele affair!

It was a lovely sunny day in October as we moved out of St Jan ter Biezen on the first "leg" of our journey to "the line."

We passed through Vlameitinghe and St Julien and, all the time, the countryside became more war-ravaged and menancing.

~~It was a great revelation to me to see large numbers of tanks lying helpless on one side in a rather marshy area, just before reaching the Henin Road.~~ The battalion stayed near the bridge in some deep dugouts on one side and a large field hospital on the other, fully staffed with doctors and nurses.

Next morning as we were getting ready to continue our journey to the line, I was stung twice by wasps in about ten minutes of each other; the place was "alive" with wasps, all of them in a semi-"intoxicated" condition.

There were a number of enemy reconnaissance planes

in the air as we made our way forward. Also, we saw several of our observation balloons brought down by enemy planes.

Previously, the weather had been hot and dry, but now, it rained heavily and by the time the attack on Passcheendale started, the whole of the battle line was one huge quagmire, bringing the attack to a stand-still. It was impossible to go on.

I saw fifty large tanks lying helpless in the mud, daily targets of "Jerry" artillery - a dead loss. At this time, our Company was very short of officers and N.C.O's. My friend, who was the Platoon Sergeant, became the officer in charge of the 16th Platoon; another friend, a Corporal was made Sergeant and I was given the job as runner for my friend, now Platoon Officer.

Whilst on our way forward, we were bombed and machine-
gunned by...

in the air as we made our way forward. Also, we saw several of our observation balloons brought down by enemy planes.

Previously, the weather had been hot and dry, but now, it rained heavily and by the time the attack on Passchendaele started the whole of the battle line was one huge quagmire bringing the attack to a stand-still. It was impossible to go on.

I saw fifty large tanks lying helpless in the mud, daily targets of "Jerry" artillery – a dead loss. At this time, our company was very short of officers and N.C.O.s. My friend, who was the Platoon Sergeant, became the officer in charge of the 16th Platoon and another friend, a corporal, was made Sergeant and I was given the job as runner for my friend, now Platoon Officer.

Whilst on our way forward, we were bombed and machine-gunned by...

by four "Gotha's" and a Brigadier's car, which had been left by the side of the road, was blown to pieces; also some wagons on a light railway near by. Some of us laid down near a stack of boxes on the side of the road during the raid, but had no idea of the danger we had been in of being blown up, if by some mischance, the boxes had been penetrated by a machine-gun bullet. The boxes contained small-arms ammunition!

The country-side everywhere, was now full of shell holes, and leaving the road now for a duck-board track, we were rather disturbed to see a body, with our regimental flashes on his uniform, lying on the track.

This turned out to be an officer's servant, one of the advance party, who had been drinking too much officer's rum. I never heard what happened to him, but he could have faced a court-martial.

The duck-board track now began to show the effects of artillery fire...

four "Gothas" and a Brigadier's car, which had been left by the side of the road, was blown to pieces; also some wagons on a light railway near by. Some of us laid down near a stack of boxes on the side of the road during the raid, but had no idea of the danger we had been in of being blown up, if by some mischance the boxes had been penetrated by a machine-gun bullet. The boxes contained small arms ammunition!

The countryside everywhere was now full of shell holes, and leaving the road now for a duck-board track, we were rather disturbed to see a body with our regimental flashes on his uniform, lying on the track.

This turned out to be an officer's servant, one of the advance party, who had been drinking too much officers' rum. I never heard what happened to him, but he could have faced a court-martial.

The duck-board track now began to show the effects of artillery fire...

many being blown clear of the track
and broken, and, presently shell-
fire was observed to be falling
on the ridge beyond. It was
now becoming dark and visibility
was poor.

This was the time of day when
the "creeping" barrages started,
trying to catch troops on the
duck-boards, moving up, perhaps,
to relieve those in the front line
during the hours of darkness.

No movement of troops could be
made in daylight and all troops
going up to occupy the front
line had to take two days'
rations with them (food and
water). They then held the line
for two days only, when they were
relieved. Things were very rough.

My friend and I were looking
for our company headquarters
everywhere it was pitch dark; now
and then a "Verey" light would
go up and we stood perfectly
still until it dropped and the
light went out. Then the darkness
seemed more intense. The stillness shattered now and then
                              by shell-fire...

many being blown clear of the track and broken, and presently shell-fire was observed to be falling on the ridge beyond. It was now becoming dark and visibility was poor.

This was the time of day when the "creeping" barrages started, trying to catch troops on the duck-boards moving up, perhaps to relieve those in the front line during the hours of darkness.

No movement of troops could be made in daylight and all troops going up to occupy the front line had to take two days' rations with them (food and water). They then held the line for two days only, when they were relieved. Things were very rough.

My friend and I were looking for our company headquarters, everywhere it was pitch dark; now and then a "Verey" light would go up and we stood perfectly still until it dropped and the light went out. Then the darkness seemed more intense, the stillness shattered now and then by shell-fire...

One could judge the direction of the front line by the "thug-thug" of the German machine-guns and the staccato sound of our own machine-guns near by.

We still hadn't found the company H.Q., so my friend said: "You stay here, Bill and I'll go and look for our H.Q. and, when I've found it, I will come back for you."

It was a frightful situation, shells "crumping" down all the time. I waited for two hours, but he didn't return. I had never liked the idea from the first, what with shell- and machine-gun fire going on all the time. No shelter, nothing but shell-holes, some of which were full of water, anything could have happened to him.

So I set off to try and find the H.Q. by myself. What a hope! I never saw a soul, except three others of our platoon, who said I must get in the shell hole with them as "Jerry" periodically put up a machine-gun barrage "to keep our heads down."

162

One could judge the direction of the front line by the "thug-thug" of the German machine-guns and the staccato sound of our own machine-guns near by.

We still hadn't found the company H.Q., so my friend said, "you stay here, Bill, and I'll go and look for our H.Q. and, when I've found it, I will come back for you."

It was a frightful situation, shells "crumping" down all the time. I waited for two hours, but he didn't return. I had never liked the idea from the first, what with shell- and machine-gun fire going on all the time. No shelter, nothing but shell-holes, some of which were full of water, anything could have happened to him.

So I set off to try and find the H.Q. by myself. What a hope! I never saw a soul except three others of our platoon who said, I must get in the shell hole with them as "Jerry" periodically put up a machine-gun barrage "to keep our heads down."

Wounded Again!

We stayed in the dug-out for two days, during which time it was almost impossible to put one's head up for a quick look round.

Our "relief" came up in twos and threes, just at dusk and we left in the same way. We were hoping to get out of the danger zone before "Jerry" started the barrages, but we were out of luck, and had only covered about a hundred yards, when down came the barrage, luckily about fifty yards to the rear of us. There wasn't even time to get down and that's how I got the shell fragment in my right leg. It had a curious effect of taking all the strength out of my leg, temporarily immobilizing me and I just had to stay where I was. My friend, Sidney, who had escaped injury, kept on calling "Come on, Bill!", but I told him to keep moving and I would come along later. . . .

19. Wounded again!

We stayed in the dug-out for two days, during which time it was almost impossible to put one's head up for a quick look around.

Our "relief" came up in twos and threes, just at dusk and we left in the same way. We were hoping to get out of the danger zone before "Jerry" started the barrages, but we were out of luck, and had only covered about a hundred yards, when down came the barrage, luckily about fifty yards to the rear of us. There wasn't even time to get down and that's how I got the shell fragment in my right leg. It had a curious effect of taking all the strength out of my leg, temporarily immobilizing me and I just had to stay where I was. My friend, Sidney, who had escaped injury, kept on calling "Come on Bill!" but I told him to keep moving and I would come along later...

Walking was impossible, so I tried "crawling", and tried to reach what appeared to be a "pillbox"; but, found, when I got inside, that it was full of Germans, casualties of recent battles, all dead and stacked from floor to ceiling.

. I found it impossible to stay in that gruesome place, and got out into the open again, first trying to get my bearings, but in the awful darkness, with shell-holes everywhere, and having to crawl along, it was a real nightmarish adventure.

In the dark, I suddenly found I had crawled into a lot of iron debris, and took shelter in, what appeared to be the boiler of the railway engine near by. As I rested, I kept looking all round to see if a spot of light appeared for a second or so.

This, I gathered, would be the battalion first-aid post, with the light showing for a second every time someone went in...

166

Wounded again!

Walking was impossible so I tried "crawling," and tried to reach what appeared to be a "pillbox," but found, when I got inside, that it was full of Germans, casualties of recent battles, all dead and stacked from floor to ceiling.

I found it impossible to stay in that gruesome place and got out into the open again, first trying to get my bearings, but in the awful darkness with shell-holes everywhere and having to crawl along, it was a real nightmarish adventure.

In the dark, I suddenly found I had crawled into a lot of iron debris and took shelter in what appeared to be the boiler of the railway engine nearby. As I rested I kept looking all round to see if a spot of light appeared for a second or so.

This, I gathered, would be the battalion first-aid post with the light showing for a second every time someone went in...

or out. Presently, I was rewarded and saw the speck of light for one second. and decided to make for this first-aid post. where I should find (I hoped) Doctor Gray and an orderly.

I carefully noted the position, but, somehow, in the darkness, crawled to a shell-hole with some Australians holding the "fort". They told me not to make a sound, only whisper as "Jerry" was only 20 yards away. They told me to turn round and go straight ahead from there and I should find the first-aid post.

They were right and I slipped inside quickly, and managed to probe out the shell fragment and put a dressing on the wound. A corporal was just going back to the battalion so they asked him to help me down, as I could not walk, very quickly.

We had only gone about 100 yards, when "Jerry" started shelling again. The Corporal shouted...

or out. Presently, I was rewarded and saw the speck of light for one second and decided to make for this first-aid post where I should find (I hoped) Doctor Gray and an orderly.

I carefully noted the position but somehow in the darkness crawled to a shell-hole with some Australians holding the "fort." They told me not to make a sound, and only whisper, as "Jerry" was only 20 yards away. They told me to turn round and go straight ahead from there and I should find the first-aid post.

They were right and I slipped inside quickly, and managed to probe out the shell fragment and put a dressing on the wound. A corporal was just going back to the battalion, so they asked him to help me down, as I could not walk very quickly.

We had only gone about 100 yards, when "Jerry" started shelling again. The Corporal shouted…

"Come on!" and disappeared into the night. I was absolutely incapable of "coming on" and just had to drag myself along at a snail's pace, when a "barrage" started on my immediate front about 200 yards away.

For a moment, I felt lost, but I reasoned that it would not do to stand still, as if the barrage suddenly lifted, it could well come down again on the spot where I was standing. At that moment some voice within me, seemed to say "keep moving," and, although it was a most terrifying experience, I had faith enough to keep walking. Sure enough, the barrage lifted and came down again in the area I had just left. To me, the incident has always seemed to possess all the ingredients of a miracle. I have never forgotten it. It is difficult to explain, but I never felt I was alone on that duck-board track. There were other incidents ...

"Come on!" and disappeared into the night. I was absolutely incapable of "coming on," and just had to drag myself along at a snail's pace, when a "barrage" started on my immediate front about 200 yards away.

For a moment, I felt lost, but I reasoned that it would not do to stand still, as if the barrage suddenly lifted, it could well come down again on the spot where I was standing. At that moment some voice within me seemed to say "keep moving!" and, although it was a most terrifying experience, I had faith enough to keep walking.

Sure enough, the barrage lifted and came down again in the area I had just left. To me, the incident has always seemed to possess all the ingredients of a miracle. I have never forgotten it. It is difficult to explain, but I never felt I was alone on that duck-board track. There were other incidents...

Later, on this long trek to base, I met one of our platoon, whose friend had been killed and, he was in such a state of mental distress, that he was just wandering about in the darkness.

x   x   x   x

My friends were all much relieved when I turned up at the camp at about 2 a.m., especially Sid who was with me when I was hit by the shell-case fragment. I laid down to "rest" in the tent, where a place had been kept for me, but it was an uneasy rest as the camp had rather an awful battering from enemy artillery fire any a good many men were wounded.

Early next morning, I was taken over to the R.A.M.C. unit and, with others who were unable to walk, put on a horse ambulance. I sat with the driver. It was a long drive to the railhead; jogging along on the Menin road; long, and with a good deal of apprehension, as I saw shells bursting on the road ahead every few minutes and worked out a cal- culation...

Wounded again!

Later, on this long trek to base, I met one of our platoon, whose friend had been killed, and he was in such a state of mental distress, that he was just wandering about in the darkness.

* * * * *

My friends were all much relieved when I turned up at the camp at about 2 a.m., especially Sid who was with me when I was hit by the shell-case fragment. I laid down to "rest" in the tent, where a place had been kept for me, but it was an uneasy rest as the camp had rather an awful battering from enemy artillery fire and a good many men were wounded.

Early next morning I was taken over to the R.A.M.C. unit and with others who were unable to walk, put on a horse ambulance. I sat with the driver. It was a long drive to the railhead; jogging along on the Menin road; long, and with a good deal of apprehension, as I saw shells bursting on the road ahead every few minutes and worked out a calculation...

using our estimated speed, the
distance still to go and the
frequency of the shell-bursts.
which resulted in a finding
which gave the answer that
the ambulance would be right
on the spot when the next shell
dropped ... and we were! ... but
on this occasion, the shell came
down about fifty yards to the
left of us ... again, it seemed
like a miracle, but, after that,
we didn't travel fast enough
for my liking. However, it
was impossible to go faster,
as some of the stretcher cases
were very serious...

The driver, who ever since we
started, had been curiously
silent, now turned to me, and
said: "We were lucky! I've
been up and down this road
many times, but never known
one to drop short like that."

I wondered if he too had
worked out where the next
shell would probably drop...

x   x   x   x

174

using our estimated speed, the distance still to go and the frequency of the shell-bursts, which resulted in a finding which gave the answer that the ambulance would be right on the spot when the next shell dropped... and we were!... but on this occasion, the shell came down about fifty yards to the left of us... again, it seemed like a miracle, but, after that, we didn't travel fast enough for my liking. However, it was impossible to go faster, as some of the stretcher cases were [very] serious...

The driver, who ever since we started, had been curiously silent, now turned to me and said: "We were lucky! I've been up and down this road many times, but never known one to drop short like that."

I wondered if he too had worked out where the next shell would probably drop...

Back in Hospital Again

Our arrival at the field hospital coincided with the overhead blast of a shrapnel shell, with its dense, black smoke, but there were no casualties, their arrival was spasmodic; sometimes several days would pass before the next one came along. No-one thought they were dangerous! but they did have a frightening effect on timid people.

Next day, we boarded the hospital train and arrived at Le Havre where we stayed the night; next day we embarked on an hospital boat and, after an uneventful journey, we all arrived at Southampton. I left the port by ambulance and arrived at an R.A.M.C. hospital at Eastleigh, a small town a short distance away.

I went home on ten days leave at the end of a month, when I had to report to the 3rd Battalion of the Norfolk Regiment at Felixstowe in Suffolk. On arrival at this depôt, the Colonel sent for me and said that they had received an order from the 18th Division in France, for my

transfer to the...

176

20. Back in hospital again

Our arrival at the field hospital coincided with the overhead blast of a shrapnel shell with its dense black smoke, but there were no casualties, their arrival was spasmodic; sometimes several days would pass, before the next one came long. No-one thought they were dangerous! but they did have a frightening effect on timid people.

Next day, we boarded the hospital train and arrived at Le Havre, where we stayed the night; next day we embarked on an hospital boat and, after an uneventful journey, we all arrived at Southampton. I left the port by ambulance and arrived at an R.A.M.C. hospital at Eastleigh, a small town a short distance away.

I went home on ten days' leave at the end of a month, when I had to report to the 3rd Battalion of the Norfolk Regiment at Felixstowe in Suffolk. On arrival at this depôt, the Colonel sent for me and said that they had received an order from the 18th Division in France, for my transfer to the...

no 2 O.C.B. at Cambridge, where I
would spend 10 months training
to be an officer, but it was a rule
of the Regiment that all those who
passed through the Battalion must
spend 6 months as a recruit instructor. I was disappointed at the
time, but I found it all good
training for what I was going to
do at Cambridge.

I was now a corporal with a
platoon of 70 Welsh lightermen from
Newport, all big, hefty men, with
a giant of a man, who had been
their ganger and, strange to say,
I have never been in charge of
a better crowd anywhere. But I was
somewhat apprehensive at first,
but I took to them and they took
to me, so we got on fine. The R.S.M.
treated well, helping me in many
ways and the Colonel smiled on
me as well.

It was a touching moment for me
when I left. The ganger said "It's a
pity you're leaving, these fellows
would go anywhere with you!"
As I walked out of the hut, they
all sang "He's a jolly good fellow!"
It was very emotional.

178

no 2 O.C.B. at Cambridge, where I would spend 10 months training to be an officer, but it was a rule of the Regiment that all those who passed through the Battalion must spend 6 months as a recruit instructor. I was disappointed at the time, but I found it all good training for what I was going to do at Cambridge.

I was now a corporal with a platoon of 70 Welsh lightermen from Newport, all big, hefty men, with a giant of a man, who had been their ganger and, strange to say, I have never been in charge of a better crowd anywhere. But I was somewhat apprehensive at first, but I took to them and they took to me, so we got on fine. The R.S.M. treated [me] well, helping me in many ways and the Colonel smiled on me as well.

It was a touching moment for me when I left. The ganger said "It's a pity you're leaving, these fellows would go anywhere with you!" As I walked out of the hut, they all sang "He's a jolly good fellow!" It was very emotional.

At Queen's College, Cambridge on an Officers' Course

A very pleasant place, with a kind of old world atmosphere; clocks on the college towers and churches all chiming the quarters and full hour, making a kind of tune all the different tones blending together. I found it very difficult to get to sleep on my first night there, but, after a time one becomes accustomed to the sound, and it has a rather restful effect.

We had lots of lectures, fair and rough note books had to be handed in every month for inspection, after the monthly examination, in which one had to gain 70 marks for a pass. Failing to do this resulted in one being sent back to their unit.

The final exam was very tough and lasted for two days; then we had the final practical exam. — on the parade ground and in the field manoeuvres. We carried the college colours in all the various branches of ...

21. At Queen's College, Cambridge on an officers' course

A very pleasant place with a kind of old world atmosphere; clocks on the college towers and churches all chiming the quarters and full hour, making a kind of tune, all the different tones blending together. I found it very difficult to get to sleep on my first night there but, after a time one becomes accustomed to the sound, and it has a rather restful effect.

We had lots of lectures, fair and rough note-books had to be handed in every month for inspection, after the monthly examination, in which one had to gain 70 marks for a pass. Failing to do this resulted in one being sent back to their unit.

The final exam was very tough and lasted for two days; then we had the final practical exam – on the parade ground and in the field manoeuvres. We carried the college colours in all the various branches of…

sport, upholding the best traditions
(I hope). There were a few, however,
who never went in for anything
and the Company Officer must have
"got wind of this, for one Saturday
morning, when the company were
all on parade, he ordered all those
engaged in sport to fall out and
form two ranks on the left.
     It was rather amusing, really,
to see a small group left, who
were not taking any part in the
college sport at all! These he
turned over to the physical instructors, with orders to keep them
busy every Saturday morning.
     In the end, they decided to
take up sport of one kind or
another, in preference to being
taken for long runs and other
kinds of physical "jerks".

     On one occasion, three-quarters
of the Company failed their monthly
exam. The Major was furious about
this and gave us a regular "dressing-
down" on parade. On returning
to my rooms, I examined the
leaflet on "Wiring" from which the
question was supposed to be...

sport, upholding the best traditions (I hope). There were a few, however, who never went in for anything and the Company Officer must have "got wind" of this, for one Saturday morning, when the company were all on parade, he ordered all those engaged in sport to fall out and form two ranks on the left.

It was rather amusing, really, to see a small group left who were not taking any part in the college sport at all. These he turned over to the physical instructors, with orders to keep them busy every Saturday morning.

In the end, they decided to take up sport of one kind or another in preference to being taken for long runs and other kinds of physical "jerks."

* * * * *

On one occasion three-quarters of the Company failed their monthly exam. The Major was furious about this and gave us a regular "dressing down" on parade. On returning to my rooms I examined the leaflet on "wiring" from which the question was supposed to be...

taken, and could find no reference to the subject mentioned
in the question. But I was
determined to get to the bottom of
the matter, so I looked in a
leaflet on wiring, marked with a
rubber stamp "obsolete" and sure
enough, I found the paragraph
from which the young lieutenant
had taken his question.

So he (Major) called three of us
to his office and asked us if anyone had a reason to submit as
to why he had failed. I waited
for a moment to see if anyone
else had anything to say, but
as all were silent and somewhat
overawed by the occasion, I said:
"I think Mr. S— set his question
from an obsolete leaflet on wiring,
sir."

Mr. S— looked as if he could
have killed me on the spot. The
Major made no comment, but
his look at Mr. S. boded ill for
that officer and he just said:
That is all, Dismiss.

Mr. S. never lost an opportunity
of trying to "catch me out" after...

184

taken, and could find no reference to the subject mentioned in the question. But I was determined to get to the bottom of the matter, so I looked in a leaflet on wiring, marked with a rubber stamp "obsolete" and sure enough found the paragraph from which the young lieutenant had taken his question.

So he (Major) called three of us to his office and asked us if anyone had a reason to submit as to why he had failed. I waited for a moment to see if anyone else had anything to say, but as all were silent and somewhat overawed by the occasion, I said: "I think Mr S------ set his question from an obsolete leaflet on Wiring, sir."

Mr S------ looked as if he could have killed me on the spot. The Major made no comment but his look at Mr S------ boded ill for that officer and he just said: That is all, dismiss.

Mr S------ never lost an opportunity of trying to "catch me out" after...

that. For instance, one day, when on manoeuvres. he was in charge of the "enemy" force and he put me in command of the attacking force.

By sending out scouts, I was able to find out just how wide his line was defended and, making a wide detour, managed to get a largish force round his flank without being detected.

While this was going on, the rest of us kept up a strong covering fire and gave the impression we were making a frontal attack.

Then our force gave a cheer and the force at the rear started firing and the "enemy" were caught between two fires.

The umpire galloped up and told Mr. S— that his party were to lay down their arms, as they were "all in the air." His rage knew no bounds and he went around shouting "It couldn't be done!"

The Sergeant - Major of our Company was . . .

that. For instance, one day, when on manoeuvres, he was in charge of the "enemy" force and he put me in command of the attacking force.

By sending out scouts, I was able to find out just how wide his line was defended and, making a wide detour, managed to get a largish force round his flank without being detected.

While this was going on, the rest of us kept up a strong covering fire and gave the impression we were making a frontal attack.

Then our force gave a cheer and the force at the rear started firing and the "enemy" were caught between two fires.

The umpire galloped up and told Mr S------ that his party were to lay down their arms as they were "all in the air." His rage knew no bounds and he went around shouting "It couldn't be done!"

* * * * *

The Sergeant-Major of our company was...

was a rather pompous individual,
and, at our morning parades,
always seemed to pick on the
same fellow. This fellow's name
was "Poundall" and he wore a
type of "glasses" which gave the
onlookers the impression he was
looking down.

As he came along to inspect
the Company his first words were
almost always "Looking on the
ground, again, Poundall!" This
Repetition of the same remark
caused a good deal of annoyance.
So the young "sparks" found out
that he had been in the "Royal
Marines, before coming to No. 2
O.C.B. at Queen's College, so they
wrote the words and put it
to music, so that it could be
sung, whilst marching at ease.
It went as follows:
   "There was a sergeant-major,
      He joined the Royal Marines;
   And when they got fed up with him,
      They sent him down to Queens.'
   When he's dead and buried,
      We'll gaze upon his mound
   And think of poor old Poundall
      Looking on the ground."

a rather pompous individual, and at our morning parades, always seemed to pick on the same fellow. This fellow's name was "Poundall" and he wore a type of "glasses" which gave the onlooker the impression he was looking down.

As he came along to inspect the Company his first words were almost always "looking on the ground again Poundall!" This repetition of the same remark caused a good deal of annoyance. So the young "sparks" found out that he had been in the Royal Marines, before coming to No. 2 O.C.B. at Queen's College, so they wrote the words and put it to music so that it could be sung, whilst marching at ease. It went as follows:

> "There was a sergeant-major
> He joined the Royal Marines;
> And when they got fed up with him,
> They sent him down to Queen's.
> When he's dead and buried,
> We'll gaze upon his mound
> And think of poor old Poundall
> Looking on the ground."

He was marching in front with the officer-in-charge and his face and neck went very red. as he turned round and said: "March to Attention!" in a loud voice. The officer also turned round with a broad grin on his face.

The point had been made, however, and I think left the Sergeant-Major in the unhappy position of not knowing what we were going to do next...

But the next incident was not far away... On the day when we normally had "fire drill", it had been pouring with rain and everywhere was dripping wet, so the powers-that-be decided not to use any water for the operation, but just to go through the motions. So the hose was just held by the operator and pointed towards the building. It was not connected with the hydrants.

One of the cadets, however, when simulating the movents, actually connected the hose. All the N.C.O's and Officers were...

He was marching in front with the officer-in-charge and his face and neck went very red, as he turned round and said: "March to Attention!" in a loud voice. The officer also turned round with a broad grin on his face.

The point had been made however and I think left the Sergeant-Major in the unhappy position of not knowing what we were going to do next...

But the next incident was not far away... on the day when we normally had "fire drill," it had been pouring with rain and everywhere was dripping wet, so the powers-that-be decided not to use any water for the operation, but just to go through the motions. So the hose was just held by the operator and pointed towards the building. It was not <u>connected</u> with the hydrants.

One of the cadets, however, when simulating the movements, actually connected the hose. All the N.C.O.s and Officers were...

on the other side of the lawn watching this "practice" when, suddenly, the hose which the cadet was holding, went stiff as the water rushed through. He turned round to see what had happened and the jet of water from the hose, caught the Sergeant-Major "amidships," knocking him over and soaking him to the skin...

This was too much for the young officers, who disappeared hurriedly into the Company office, while the N.C.O's went to the assistance of the Sergeant-Major who was already clamouring for the blood of the perpetrater, incidentally, a cadet named Fleming.

The Sergeant-Major then made a great mistake, he marched a young man named Bruce into the Company office, who bore a passable resemblance to Fleming and introduced him to the Major as the cadet who had wilfully turned the water on and soaked him with water.

On being asked by the Major if he had anything to say...

on the other side of the lawn watching this "practice" when, suddenly, the hose which the cadet was holding went stiff as the water rushed through. He turned round to see what had happened and the jet of water from the hose, caught the Sergeant-Major "amidships," knocking him over and soaking him to the skin...

This was too much for the young officers who disappeared hurriedly into the Company office, while the N.C.O.s went to the assistance of the Sergeant-Major who was already clamouring for the blood of the perpetrator, incidentally, a cadet named Fleming.

The Sergeant-Major then made a great mistake, he marched a young man named Bruce into the Company office, who bore a passable resemblance to Fleming and introduced him to the Major as the Cadet who had wilfully turned the water on and soaked him with water.

On being asked by the Major if he had anything to say...

Bruce replied that his name was "Bruce, not Fleming", whilst the Sergeant-Major insisted he was Fleming. However, at that time the culprit walked into the office and explained that the whole affair was quite an accident and expressed his regret.

The Major accepted his explanation as quite adequate and the matter was closed. The private feelings of the C.S.M. were never known, but his look boded ill for Fleming, if he should ever "put a foot wrong".

x x x x

In our leisure time, we went on week-end boating parties and fishing in the river "Granta". Sports days and river frolics. Cross-country runs, tennis and football in winter I once played at centre-half against Cambridge University. After what I had been through in France, it was easily the best holiday I ever had. It was early in November, when I was just about to give a lecture on "Anti-Gas Measures".

Bruce replied that his name was "Bruce," not Fleming, whilst the Sergeant-Major insisted he was Fleming. However, at that time, the culprit walked into the office and explained that the whole affair was quite an accident and expressed his regret.

The Major accepted his explanation as quite adequate and the matter was closed. The private feelings of the C.S.M. were never known, but his look boded ill for Fleming, if he should ever "put a foot wrong."

* * * * *

In our leisure time, we went on week-end boating parties and fishing in the river "Granta." Sports days and river frolics, cross-country runs, tennis and football in winter. I once played at centre-half against Cambridge University. After what I had been through in France, it was easily the best holiday I ever had. It was early in November, when I was just about to give a lecture on "Anti-Gas Measures"…

to the assembled company, when a "runner" arrived from Battalion Headquarters to say that I had a baby daughter. Someone else took my place as the Lecturer and I was allowed a "pass" for four days to go and see her.

As I was riding down to the City of Norwich to register her birth, all the sirens went on and everyone thought an air raid was imminent.

Actually, it was to announce the "Armistice." So, it was all over! and when I returned to my unit, there was a good deal less discipline and more recreation than was allowed in war-time.

I stayed with the Unit until the middle of 1919, when I left for home, after being put on Reserve, relinquishing my Commission in 1922 ... And so, on to Civilian life again, with all its hazards and uncertainties...

to the assembled company, when a "runner" arrived from Battalion Headquarters to say that I had a baby daughter. Someone else took my place as the Lecturer and I was allowed a "pass" for four days to go and see her.

As I was riding down to the City of Norwich to register her birth all the sirens went on and everyone thought an air raid was imminent.

Actually, it was to announce the "Armistice." So it was all over! and when I returned to my unit, there was a good deal less discipline and more recreation than was allowed in war-time.

I stayed with the Unit until the middle of 1919, when I left for home after being put on Reserve, relinquishing my commission in 1922... and so on to civilian life again, with all its hazards and uncertainties...

Return to "Curvy" Street
May 1919

Hopes of a brighter future were running high at this time. Wages were good and jobs were plentiful. Politicians were forward-looking and Lloyd-George had promised to "build a countries fit for heroes to live in."

So the time passed for two years, when the rumblings of a post-war depression began to be heard. Firms had promised the men who joined up in 1914 that their jobs would be available for them after the war. Most employers honoured their pledges, but many did not. This resulted in the forming of The British Legion and other organisations to see that the ex-service men received a fair deal.

The short period of prosperity soon passed and Lloyd Georges promise of "a country fit for heroes to live in," was changed by a disappointed people to "You have to be a hero to live in it.

Unemployment reached its highest level...

22. Return to "Civvy" Street, May 1919

Hopes of a brighter future were running high at this time. Wages were good and jobs were plentiful. Politicians were forward-looking and Lloyd George had promised to "build a country fit for heroes to live in."

So the time passed for two years, when the rumblings of a post-war depression began to be heard. Firms had promised the man who joined up in 1914 that their jobs would be available for them after the war. Most employers honoured their pledges but many did not. This resulted in the forming of the British Legion and other organisations to see that the ex-service men received a fair deal.

The short period of prosperity soon passed and Lloyd George's promise of a "country fit for heroes to live in" was changed by a disappointed people to "you have to be a hero to live in it."

Unemployment reached its highest level...

but very few ever benefited from
signing on at the "bureau", as it
was an order from the government "that only the very minimum
of staff should be discharged,
but kept on a basis of three days
at work and three days off.
Thus, the official numbers of
unemployed would appear to be
moderate. The reason those who
were working never drew any
benefit was because of a rule
made especially for the occasion.
This rule stated that a man
had to be totally unemployed
for six consecutive days. to
qualify for benefit.
The three-day employees never
qualified for benefit, because of
this rule.
There was great hardship everywhere causing strikes, food riots,
hunger marches - the lot. At this
time I became a 3-day man. My
firm had already sacked all the
employees over 40. I was married
and had two small children
under "five", so I had to do something to supplement the income.
In my off days

200

but very few ever benefitted from signing on at the "bureau," as it was an order from the government "that only the very minimum of staff should be discharged, but kept on a basis of three days of work and three days off.

Thus, the official numbers of unemployed would appear to be moderate. The reason those who were working never drew any benefit was because of a rule made especially for the occasion. This rule stated that a man had to be totally unemployed for six consecutive days to qualify for benefit.

The three-day employees never qualified for benefit because of this rule.

There was great hardship everywhere causing strikes, food riots, hunger marches – the lot. At this time I became a 3-day man. My firm had already sacked all the employees over 40. I was married and had two small children under "five," so I had to do something to supplement the income. In my off days...

I went round getting orders for tickets and showcards and spent half the night executing the orders. This was a lot of work for little money, but it was a great help.

Once, there was a job going, with the Education Authorities of Norwich who advertised for a School Attendance Officer." I applied and was asked to provide three references: The Deputy Chief Constable of Norfolk supplied one, a director of Boardmans the Architects another and the third came from the minister of our church. I did not get the job, because the advertisement was only to conform to a rule "that the vacancy must be advertised in the local press.

I found out later that the post had been filled, some time before the announcement in the press. I feel it was outrageous for the Education Secretary to ask one to supply three references when it was already decided who should fill this...

202

I went round getting orders for tickets and showcards and spent half the night executing the orders. This was a lot of work for little money but it was a great help.

Once, there was a job going with the Education Authorities of Norwich who advertised for a School Attendance Officer.

I applied and was asked to provided three references: the Deputy chief Constable of Norfolk supplied one; a director of Boardman's the Architects another and the third came from the minister of our church. I did not get the job because the advertisement was only to conform to a rule "that the vacancy must be advertised in the local press."

I found out later that the post had been filled, sometime before the announcement in the press. I feel it was outrageous for the Education Secretary to ask one to supply three references when it was already decided who should fill this...

vacancy. It was impossible to break down this "closed shop" business".

one day, much later, I decided to go and see my father at Palgrave, near Diss and, at the same time, visit an old friend of mine, at Diss, who had a printing business, and see if he could find me a regular job. During the course of our conversation, I smiled and said to him: "I dont suppose ~~you~~ want a good man to run ~~your~~ business for you?"

To my great surprise, he said: "As a matter of fact, I do!" and terms were agreed. In a month's time after that, I was working a full week again, in Diss of all places, where I knew almost everyone.

I joined the Methodist Church; also was a foundation member of the British Legion. Later, I served on the Court of Referees and obtained a paid job as clerk to the Old Age Pension Sub-
Committee...

Committee...

204

vacancy. It was impossible to break down this "closed shop" business.

* * * * *

One day, much later, I decided to go and see my father at Palgrave near Diss and, at the same time, visit an old friend of mine at Diss who had a printing business, and see if he could find me a regular job.

During the course of our conversation, I smiled and said to him: "I don't suppose you want a good man to run your business for you?"

To my great surprise he said: "As a matter of fact, I do!" and terms were agreed. In a month's time after that, I was working a full week again, in Diss of all places, where I knew almost everyone.

I joined the Methodist church; also was a foundation member of the British Legion. Later, I served on the Court of Referees and obtained a paid job as clerk to the Old Age Pension Sub-Committee...

Later I was appointed as the Lecturer in Typography, including Printing Design and Lay-out at the Norwich College and School of Art, a post I held for fifteen years, including the war years until 1943.

It was in 1936 that I lost my leg and we moved to Norwich, and for the period up to 1939, I had three operations, I continued at the College as soon as I had recovered, having a taxi to fetch me from my old firm (where I was in August 1914 and where I was now a press reader) and take me to the College and, at the end of the classes, fetch me again and take me home.

Return to "Civvy" Street, May 1919

Later I was appointed as the Lecturer in Typography, including Printing Design and Layout at the Norwich College and School of Art, a post I held for fifteen years, including the war years until 1943.

* * * * *

It was in 1936 that I lost my leg and we moved to Norwich, and for the period up to 1939 I had three operations. I continued at the College as soon as I had recovered, having a taxi to fetch me from my old firm (where I was in August 1914 and where I was now a press reader) and take me to the College and, at the end of the classes, fetch me again and take me home.

Editor's note: we conclude William Bennett's memoir at this point, with his remark that it was in 1936 that he lost his leg. This was the long-term consequence of the shrapnel wound he received at Passchendaele in 1917 (see chapters 18 and 19). His diary ends soon after the above, with a few details of the second world war and of domestic and local affairs.

Opposite:
Portrait of William C. Bennett, after being commissioned as an officer, painted probably 1919 or later by his brother-in-law Ernest Faircloth. We have not found any early photograph of William as a young man or as a private soldier.

wu/ψ